TECHNOLOGY CONSULTANT FAST TRACK

TECHNOLOGY CONSULTANT FAST TRACK

HOW TO GET YOUR DREAM JOB IN IT CONSULTING

EETU NIEMI, PhD

Paperback ISBN: 979-8-7213-6953-7

PRAISE FOR THE BOOK

"The book gives a strong and realistic description of IT consultancy. Thus, every IT student should read the book before they graduate as it will increase their probability of landing a dream job." **Samuli Pekkola, Professor, PhD, in Information Systems Sciences, Tampere University**

"The book gives insight into technology consulting and provides great tips for job search. I believe it will be very valuable when I start looking for a position in IT. The section on how to stand out as a candidate for a job was an eyeopener." **Saku Sikiö, Information Systems Student, University of Jyväskylä**

"This is the book I would have needed on the verge of graduation!" **Teijo Kelander, MSc, Quality Consultant and Agile Coach**

"If you are serious about IT consultancy as a profession, this book is a must-read! As a recruiter, I would prefer that applicants would better understand what this is all about." **Petteri Laamanen, MSc, CEO & Founder, Coala**

"This book gave me valuable insights into the IT consultant's working life, making it easier to consider the pros and cons in relation to my own values and goals." **Janita Kingelin, MSc, Marketing Manager, SoulCore**

CONTENTS

PREFACE

A Helicopter View

The client was so happy. Yes, we had billed two Maybachs worth of consulting hours in the past few months, but they were worth it. My consulting assignment was about to finish and something completely different was to begin. At that moment, I had been employed by a well-known, global consulting giant for three-and-a-half years. By that time, I had worked in over a dozen projects, with almost as many clients.

Now, looking out from the helicopter window, I see the lights of Helsinki, quickly falling behind as the aircraft begins its 15-minute trip towards Estonia, the southern neighbor of Finland. I am no stranger to flying but have flown in a helicopter only once before. Flying at the scant altitude of only 2 000 ft over the dark sea is an unforgettable experience. Save for the occasional light from a passing ship, there is only water to see.

The recent history of the relatively young helicopter connection also spiced things up. The route had just been reopened after a copter plummeted to the sea six years ago, killing everyone on board. Our team of consultants was now flying another make, but I was not sure if that was supposed to be reassuring. Anyway, it was difficult not to feel excited.

We were going to celebrate a successful project in style. Having gotten bored of the restaurant scene in Helsinki, we instead took a helicopter to Tallinn, Estonia (just 80 kilometers away over the Gulf of Finland) and dined in the best restaurant in town. This time, the menu consisted of modern Asian delicacies. The food was so good we ended up ordering an extra round of the best courses.

Of course, I had not come to IT consulting for the sake of helicopter rides and great dinners (although such experiences are a more than welcome plus). But my years at the consulting giant had shown me that I love IT consulting. Even if we had zero helicopter rides and just ate broccoli, I would name IT consulting as my dream profession without skipping a beat.

This was in December 2011. Finally, I had landed a project of my own. I had learned more in that relatively short time than I had ever dreamed possible, growing from a relatively junior note-taker and documenter to managing a small team and handling customer relations independently. Working with the team was fun, and my supervisor was just amazing. He really knew how to keep his people happy.

Now, I knew what IT solution implementation projects were all about, having contributed to them in several different positions, such as designer and tester. I had worked with senior managers and executives in strategic architecture projects. I had gotten a public commendation and a bottle of champagne as the new joiner of the year coming directly from the university (literally true).

That moment was also three and a half years after I had refused a hard-won, paid PhD student position in a university and put my PhD thesis on hold, to change to a completely new career in IT consulting—as a surprise to all. Looking back, it was probably one of the best decisions I have made in my life.

It had not been an easy ride. Even with some client contact and project management experience from the research project, the learning curve in the years to come had been steep. Nevertheless, I had stood up to the challenges and gained experience one would probably not get in any other profession.

A Change of Gears

A year or so after that restaurant trip to Tallinn, there would be another major change. After working at the company for five years, I decided it was time to move on. I would be changing to a three-person (at the time, counting me) consulting firm called Coala to do solely architecture consulting (or so I thought at the time). In terms of getting that position, the experience was totally different from the traditional way of applying to the consulting giant. More about my job search in chapters to come.

At the time of writing, I have worked in IT consulting for over ten years. I have been involved with almost 30 client organizations and 50 projects. I have seen parts of the Finnish public sector, including a couple of ministries and assorted national security and safety authorities (that have to remain anonymous), as well as some of the largest companies.

After being employed at Coala for four years, I made a partner (the first and still the only employee to have done it). At the global consulting giant, I was invited to travel to the US to join to teach a two-week core consulting course for a few hundred new joiners. I have been invited to present at industry events in Finland, the largest boasting more than 300 participants.

There have also been a few surprises along this journey. While attending a core consulting course near Chicago, Illinois, I met my partner, with whom I have two children. We took turns flying to meet each other for six years every month or so—before finally settling in Helsinki. In the end, I also earned my PhD for my work on enterprise architecture, ten years after initiating the work (not an easy feat to do while engaged in full-time consulting work). In addition to two cities in Finland, my studies took me to live in the UK and Germany.

After all these years in the field, I can still say that IT consulting is a great profession. If you are looking for a rewarding and interesting job that does not suck the life out of you—while still getting compensated adequately—IT consulting is an excellent option. You can have a life that you want without giving everything to your work. Of course, for this to happen, you need to find a good company and a job that is a good fit for you *and* convince them to hire you. That is where this book comes in.

1. INTRODUCTION

Why Did I Write This Book?

IT consulting as a profession is somewhat unknown to people in high school and even in graduate school. Instead, if you are interested in IT, you will probably think about becoming an internal employee in some company or in the public sector—and working as an IT expert or manager for your own organization only. I, for one, did not know what consulting was about until years later.

I want to remedy that for my part and tell you about the amazing variety of opportunities the field of IT consulting offers and shoot down some of the misconceptions. I want you to know what it is like to work in the field. As a consultant, you could be working similar to that of an internal employee but using your expertise to benefit many clients. There are suitable positions in the field for many different kinds of personalities and preferences.

I also want to share my experience in getting an IT consultant position. During the years I have worked in the field, I have seen people get hired and fired. I have had numerous discussions and interviews with others (including recruiters, IT consultants, and people looking for a job) and learned from them. I have helped friends and acquaintances to get a foothold in the field — and want to do you a similar favor.

This book can help you whether you are about to finish your studies and are looking for your first job, or already working and considering a career change. Of course, there can be many reasons for considering a swap to IT consulting. Personally, I left my promising career in the university because, after all, I wanted to do something practical — instead of laboring on my PhD, alone in my chamber. And frankly, the compensation was bad (besides, I also hated the office politics).

Even if I did not get into my first IT consulting position directly after getting my degree, I still know how burdensome a job search can be. I have sent out dozens of job applications without getting picked — even for an interview. That is how it was for me before getting that position in the university and numerous times before searching for a summer job. I want to help you avoid the mistakes people (including me) often make in their job search.

I will tell you what qualifications are the most useful and what you should know about your preferences and personality before applying. By following this advice, you can make a better choice on which companies to apply to. It will also help you to stand out as a candidate and avoid the pitfalls in work contracts. As a result, you can get a job that is the best jumpstart for your career as an IT consultant. And you will probably also earn more.

What Is This Book About?

This book takes you on a journey to the exciting world of IT consulting and shows you how to get a job that you really want in the field.

IT consultants are professionals with varied, and not only technical, expertise. You do not have to be a computer geek who wrote his or her first program at the age of five. You do not even have to have a master's in Computer Science. Background in business can be equally valuable in IT consulting.

There are a plethora of assignments IT consultants work on, from developing new IT solutions for Fortune 500 companies to creating cloud strategies for the public sector. Digitalization is here to stay, so there is plenty of work to be done. The work is not only about technology either. With modern corporations such as Amazon and Facebook, it is hard to tell where business ends and technology starts. IT and business can be thoroughly intertwined. Also IT consultants can do work with a heavy emphasis on business, such as business process improvement and service design. Not to mention strategic IT consulting work.

Even the most technically oriented coder needs to understand the business to some extent to create a useful IT solution. And as consulting is largely about interaction and communication, interpersonal skills are crucial for any consultant. Still, you do not have to be a sleek motormouth to succeed in the field.

What Is This Book Not About?

This is not a book about management or strategic consulting. That kind of work is carried out by, for example, the prestigious Big Three consulting companies—McKinsey & Company, Boston Consulting Group, and Bain & Company. Although it may be hard to distinguish between IT consulting, it is clear to those working in the field. It is mostly a cultural difference. Management consulting is traditionally characterized by high-visibility work, long hours, and strict timelines. IT consulting is often (but not always) more laid back and has a technological twist. Neither is this book about consulting in the world of construction.

This book is also not about consultants doing solely coaching, professional speaking, or training—even though all of these may be part of an IT consultant's job. IT consulting is about creating different deliverables, such as designs and working software—not only about presenting and entertaining clients.

There are tons of books, training courses, and internet resources on finding a job. I will not repeat what others have written about, for example, searching for potential employers, writing applications, handling an interview, or creating a CV or resume. Rather, I will focus on things that

I have found important through my experience and what I have heard from others.

Once you get your first IT consultant position, your journey is far from finished. To succeed, you will need to find your dream role and cultivate yourself as an IT consultant. Finding the secret sauce of succeeding in the field is a topic for a book on its own.

Finally, the book is not about self-employing yourself in consulting. It teaches you how to get a job as an employee in a company, not setting up your own business. For those interested in entrepreneurship, this might be a viable option, especially for the ones who already have some consulting experience under their belts. Still, startups are not for everyone. This is also a topic in its own right, and you will find plenty of books and other resources on it. For example, Dr. Alan Weiss has many excellent books on the subject.

What Do You Find in This Book?

The rest of the book consists of the following six chapters:

- **Chapter 2** "Know the Advantages" tells why you should consider a career as an IT consultant and outlines some behaviors and traits that do not fit well in the industry.
- **Chapter 3** "Know the Consulting Business" takes you on tour in the world of IT consulting. This chapter helps you to know the industry before ap-

plying for a job there. It gives an overview of the different tasks IT consultants do and the roles they work in. Feel free to skip this chapter if you are already familiar with the IT consulting business.

- **Chapter 4** "Know the Companies" introduces you to different kinds of IT consulting companies. You should know their characteristics to make an informed choice on what kind of company to apply to. While entry-level applicants cannot go much wrong by choosing one of the large, well-known consultancies, other options may be better for your working style and other preferences.

- **Chapter 5** "Know the Secrets of Landing Your Dream Job" teaches you how to apply for your first IT consultant position. You will find out what kind of background you need to get into the business. You will learn what you should know about your preferences and personality before sending out any job applications. Different ways of applying to an IT consultant job are also presented. You will learn to find and evaluate potential employers. There are also tips for making your application stand out of the crowd and acing the job interview. And finally, you will get an idea of what to expect as a newcomer in an IT consultancy.

- **Chapter 6** "Stories and Advice from the Front Line" presents real-life stories and advice from IT consultants working in the field. You will get an idea of how the working life can be for an IT consultant.

- **Chapter 7** "Skip the Book & Let's Go for Sodas" sends you out on your IT consulting journey with some final pieces of advice.

2. KNOW THE ADVANTAGES

Why Would I Want to Be an IT Consultant?

I will begin this chapter by pointing out why I want to be an IT consultant. It brings out nicely many of the advantages of choosing this kind of career. We will take a closer look at the advantages later in this chapter. But before making your choice, you must consider your other options. We will look at those as well.

What do I like the most about my job? I would have to say the variety of work. Working as a consultant, every new project and client brings something new. Even in a specialty like enterprise architecture, there is a lot of different work to do. I usually have several projects going on simultaneously, so I do not have to work on the same tasks every day. There are also opportunities for contributing my company's marketing, sales, and service development efforts. So, there is a good amount of change.

Freedom of organizing my own work comes in as a close second. I have a lot of say in how I organize my own work. Of course, I have deadlines and calendars of client representatives to consider, but there is still considerable freedom. Flexible work arrangements are an obvious benefit as well. There is a nice mix of teamwork and independent work.

I am also delighted with the learning opportunities. Typically, learning happens by doing, without paying much attention to it. Architecture is, among others, about documenting what the client has and how things work at the client. So, I usually end up knowing parts of the client business inside out. There is also the occasional new software tool to learn. There might not be so much time left over from client work for attending training courses. But I am still free to do so when an interesting one comes up. My employer also supports my personal growth, such as finalizing my PhD thesis. Lately, I have gotten tremendous support for writing this book.

I have not said anything yet about the compensation package. Granted, my name is not on the people-with-highest-income lists they publish every November in the papers (in Finland, everyone's tax information is public). Still, I get along very well. According to the latest wage income statistics, more than 90 % of Finland's employees earn less than me (I, for one, would be interested to know just how much more, but the statistic does not include numbers for higher percentages). After paying for the (not insignificant) expenses, there is plenty left over for investing and hobbies. I also get useful benefits. Free basic healthcare always has to be provided by employers in Finland, but we have better-than-usual coverage. For example, I get dental and massage for free—which is not so usual around here. Company-paid phone and internet access are handy. Tax-supported lunch, sports, culture, and commuting benefits go without saying.

Only knowing the compensation does not tell you whether it is low or high. You must also consider what you have to do for it. It is exceedingly important that I can work in a position and role that suits me. Being in an expert position is exactly what I want. I do not want to supervise other people or be responsible for their work. I do not want to give up any more of my free time to my work as I absolutely must. And most of all, I do not want to be on call if there is an emergency at work. Instead, I want to get my kids from kindergarten in time and spend some time with them every day. I want to have some time of my own. The typical work time per day is 7.5 hours in Finland. That is how much I work. Then, I am completely off. I very seldom get distracted with work-related things in my free time.

Of course, there would be other possible employment opportunities for me. For example, there are enterprise architect positions in large organizations. I could probably squeeze out 10 to 20 % more salary in a perfectly matched position. But then, I would be working in the same organization every day, working on the same subject matter. There would be less freedom and more red tape (bureaucracy).

For me, being an IT consultant works out beautifully. But let's find out if it can do the same for you.

What Are Your Options?

The question of whether being an IT consultant is a good choice, of course, comes down to "compared to what?" Depending on your situation, you have several options ahead of you. Only one of them is a career in IT consulting. But why should you choose that path?

Let's first look at what you can do. If you are studying now, you have all the world open before you. After graduation, you can apply to whatever position interests you. It may or may not be something related to what you studied. You can accept a position in your university or college. You can continue your studies towards, for example, a PhD. You can even be lured away from your studies to work.

An Internal Employee or a Consultant?

Your first choice is between working as an internal employee or as a consultant. As an internal employee, you work for your own employer rather than for its clients. To make things more complicated, there are also internal employees in consultancies and internal consultants in organizations. Go figure.

For example, if you are interested in IT, you could apply to an internal IT position in some company that you know. You could be, for example, a developer, a systems analyst, or an IT support specialist. If you are inclined more towards the business, there are also plenty of options for a career, for example in sales, production, human resources (HR), or finance. Of course, you can also select a position in a public sector or even a third sector organization (a nonprofit). The sectors have their differences and suit different kinds of people.

Or you could be an IT consultant. In the next section, I will compare working as an internal employee to working as a consultant. If consulting is something you know you would like to do anyway, I would suggest getting yourself directly into a consultancy. There is no need to get experience as an internal employee in a business or IT-related position first—if that is not something you specifically want to do. Sure, it provides valuable industry experience. Your clients will probably appreciate that you have also been on their side of the table. But it is not absolutely required. You will get to know enough about your consulting clients and their business regardless. And much more—and faster.

Change Jobs—or Not

If you are currently working, you also have a lot of options. Maybe you have set a strong direction for your career by your choices so far, or maybe there is more flexibility. Having work experience obviously makes it easier to get into many positions. You can even choose to go back to school and maybe then consider a career in consulting. It is up to you.

Still, changing into IT consulting from your current job is not something you should do lightly. In the section "Should You Really Change to IT Consulting?", I will tell you what you should consider. If you are one of the really experienced folks, be sure also to check the section "Do Seasoned Professionals Fit into Consulting?" below.

What Kind of Consultant (if Any)?

Even if you know that you are born to be a consultant, you still must select what kind of consultant you want to become. As brought out in the previous chapter, there are many kinds of consultants. Here, I will focus on the differences between management consultants and IT consultants. Both are relevant options for individuals with a background in either IT or business. But I still will try to convince you why a career in IT consulting is a better choice in the section "Why Not Go into Management Consulting Instead?"

Please also check the last section in this chapter. There, I will outline the behaviors and attitudes that do not make a good IT consultant. IT consulting is not for everyone, and it is also important to consider whether this kind of work suits you.

Why Not Become an Internal Employee?

There are plenty of business and IT-oriented positions that have nothing to do with consulting. This kind of position is probably the one that people usually have in mind when considering where to work after graduation. I have a hunch that few people consider a career in consulting—if they do not know any better.

IT consultants and internal employees work with the same subject matter (such as building and maintaining IT solutions), but that is about where the commonalities end. For people with a specific mindset, a consulting career brings opportunities offered by few positions for internal employees.

If you want to have it easy at work, you might have luck finding an internal employee position with low expectations. These are probably harder and harder to come by. Still, I have met a couple of people whose only value to their organization seems to be heat generation (the heat generated by the human body has a small impact on heating costs, which creates some value in countries with long and cold winters).

On the other hand, plenty of employees work like hell and get stressed in the crossfire of conflicting demands. In large global companies, employees have meetings at strange times because of different time zones. IT experts and managers must divide their attention between many projects, internal processes, routine meetings, and office politics. Many client employees I have met during my career spend most of their workday in meetings, having little time for anything else. Especially for those with management responsibility, workdays can get long. Some professionals (including, for example, those working in finance) may even have to put in more working hours than management consultants.

Some of the problems in today's workplaces seem to be that there is so much to do, yet a lack of focus on what is important. Being a consultant brings the necessary focus, at least. Consultants are usually hired to apply their expertise for a particular problem in a specific project. They can focus on that and avoid most of the other stuff organizations throw at their employees. As a consultant, you can do what you were hired to do. If you enjoy, for example, coding or creating designs, you can focus on doing what you love.

However, you will not find an easy position in consulting. Consultants have a different set of expectations that can seem burdensome to some people. As a consultant, the client pays big money for your services, so you *must* deliver. Both your client and your employer are breathing down at your neck. Consulting is a service business, so you have to be comfortable with that as well. Jobs with a heavy focus on serving the customer are not for everyone. You must also adapt quickly to every new project and client. You must learn the specifics of the client and its needs. You may even have to learn a completely new industry or technology. You will definitely need to step out of your comfort zone.

But the high expectations come with benefits. You will learn on the go, so it happens pretty much automatically. After a while, you learn to use your time efficiently, focus on the essential, and gain plenty of useful knowledge. You will see many different projects, industries, client organizations, cities, and even countries. The subject matter changes by the project and client. There are plenty of opportunities to meet people and network if you choose to.

As an internal employee, you will often work at the same office and see the same people every day. The details may change with each new task, but the bulk of the subject matter keeps the same. Depending on your personality, you might get bored or fed up. Of course, there are also great internal IT positions, but IT consultants get more variety and learning opportunities in general.

Why Not Go Into Management Consulting Instead?

Management consulting, especially in the largest and most well-known consulting companies, is known for high expectations, long workdays, and almost inhuman timelines. Management consultants work between 50 to 80 hours per week (on average) instead of the normal 40 hours. This means that during the "quiet" times, you might only work normal hours (or less). But when it gets hectic, you might have to log even 16 hours per day. Sometimes, you also have to sacrifice a Saturday or Sunday (or even both) for your work. Consider, just how effective can you be after you have already worked for, say, 10 hours in a row—and been doing crazy hours since forever? In this business, there are not enough hours in the week to do much else than work. Still, to be fair, it is not like this in *all* management consulting firms.

Management consulting projects are often high-profile. The consultants work directly with the C-level executives. Projects are small, so everyone's work is critical. Projects and clients change often. Some management consultants may spend more time in hotel rooms in various cities than at home. Naturally, this also comes with matching compensation, visibility, and ample learning opportunities. Some people obviously are comfortable with these conditions (at least for a while). But many others do not want to live only on high-visibility work and caffeine.

Generally, IT consulting is significantly more laid-back. The subject matter is "only" IT, which does not necessarily get much C-level visibility. You might be only one of the many consultants working for the client, so there is less pressure on you. You may even dress less formally, as you seldom meet individuals of the senior management. A day's work can usually be finished in the normal eight hours or so (barring a looming project deadline or occasional emergency). You might even get paid for overtime. However, if you are a manager, you will probably need to put in more hours than those working in expert positions.

Large-scale IT projects take years to complete, and there is usually new work to be done after that at the same client. So, IT consultants can work for several years at the same client. There is stability if you want it. When doing advisory kind of IT consulting, there is probably much more change.

Travel needs, of course, depend on your company, clients, and geography. If you choose your employer and clients right, you can get around with little traveling (if you wish so). Of course, you may need to move to be able to work in your favorite IT consultancy (as I did). The largest consultancies are usually located in large cities, anyway. I work in a small country's capital city, which means that most potential clients are situated close by. Crossing the city limit on a work trip is an infrequent occasion indeed. My one-way commute has taken about 20 minutes since 2012 (and I walk to work). That suits me fine.

Do not get me wrong. You are expected to and will need to work hard in IT consulting. This does not necessarily mean longer than normal hours. Still, you are expected to give 110 % when working in a client engagement. And there will be plenty of challenges. Still, IT consulting can be a friendly business for your work-life balance—*if* you work in a fitting role and find an employer that understands the importance of employee well-being. But beware, there are also firms in IT consulting that expect you to log more than standard hours in the long term. The more important it is to consider carefully where you want to work.

Do You Get Rich as an IT Consultant?

Some studies say that millennials may not hold compensation as high as the previous generations. Whether you value compensation highly or not, getting appropriate payment for your efforts does not hurt. For me, compensation expresses the respect my employer has for my work. Getting a high enough compensation also means that I can work less—if I want to.

The good news is that IT consulting is generally a profitable business. There can, of course, be huge differences between consultancies. The big names land the largest contracts, but also smaller companies can do very well in their own niches. Even consultancies selling IT generalists by the boatload can do very well. The projects tend to be long, and there is a lot of work to be billed. Granted, the rates are higher in management consulting. But also IT consultants with sought-after skills can have high rates (within reason). Still, there are very few IT consulting superstars who can ask for almost any rate.

The interesting thing is that consultancies actually make the most money with their junior consultants. Their salaries are relatively low. Even though their rates may be lower than for those with more experience, they are not *so much* lower. This is good news for young individuals looking for a job: IT consultancies are constantly hiring new entry-level employees. Also, job security is pretty good, as IT consultants seem to have work regardless of the occasional downturn. On the other hand, consultants are often the first people struggling client organizations will throw out.

How does this success then translate to the compensation of an individual IT consultant? I must break it out for you. It is a slow road to riches as an employee in an IT consultancy. But the same is also true for management consulting and almost every internal employee position. And if you live in a country with relatively high and progressive taxation (such as Finland), it is anyway challenging to get rich just by working. It helps if you are the chief executive officer (CEO) of a large consultancy, the main owner of a very successful consulting firm, or an investor.

As said, the starting salary for an IT consultant fresh out from university is not so high. It may not be much more than you would get in some other entry-level position. Still, it is a real salary that you can live with (if your expenses are reasonable, that is). And if you get into the right company, in the right role, and do your job well, your wage curve can be steep. Experienced IT consultants can get by very comfortably. For example, my current annual salary is almost exactly double what I initially earned as an IT consultant.

Of course, there are large differences in the level of compensation between different countries and companies. Even individuals doing similar work in the same IT consulting company may have different salaries. So, I cannot make any promises on your salary as an IT consultant. But I can tell you this: find your niche (or learn to be an excellent IT generalist) and a company that needs your talents, and you will be paid well.

You can, of course, also find such a place in the right position as an internal employee. But it may also be that you must take on management responsibility to get similar compensation as an IT consultant working as an expert. You must consider if you really want to be a manager. Also, the best management consulting firms will probably pay you more. But before rushing to any conclusions, you must compare the hours you need to work to get that money. If you must log in twice as many hours as an IT consultant, one-third more in salary (for example) does not sound so good after all.

How About Michelin Star Restaurants and Helicopter Rides?

I have had my share of lavish dinners, limo rides, and other rare experiences. In the IT consulting industry, you can, too. That is, if you work for a profitable consultancy with a culture of keeping its employees happy (or at least showing off to its employees). Even if the crazy days of the 2000s dot-com bubble are long gone, many IT consulting companies still use the money to give memorable and fun experiences to their employees.

There are plenty of opportunities for a good party in the industry. There are the usual Christmas and summer parties and other company events for the whole workforce. Also, there may be parties and events organized by your organizational unit. There are the sale-close parties and parties held during and after training courses and seminars.

A typical company party I attended at the consulting giant was held at some of the finer event venues and involved a buffet dinner, semi-open bar, various performers, and later, a disco. At Coala, we usually go to one of the fine-dining restaurants for a many-course dinner. Occasionally, there are also other activities. Thus far, I have dined in three restaurants with a Michelin star (so there still are a few new such places to visit in Helsinki), and countless other great eateries.

Sometimes, companies really want to put on a show at such events. At the consulting giant, I was once in an event with a huge ballroom full of people, an open bar, and a life-size ice tiger in the middle of the room (this was when such a theme was still topical). The Christmas party was usually held at one of the finest venues in Helsinki, had a dress code, and the CEO took time to shake hands with everyone on arrival. Once, we arrived at such an event in a limo (limo rides are not such a commodity in Finland as they are in, say, the US).

At least in the larger companies, it is typical to have *outings* in projects, at least once per project. Projects have different amounts of money to spend for this kind of thing. Still, usually it is enough for some sporty or non-sporty activity and a fine dinner. Projects may also have other nice customs for celebrating. In one, it was customary to have champagne at the end of each sprint (development cycle). Even clients sometimes take the time (and money) to organize something, but it is probably not so spectacular compared to your own company's events.

The activity does not always have to be bowling and drinking beer (actually, I have done that only four times connected with work, but at least on two continents). There may also be things that you have never done before, would not even think of doing, or at least would not pay your own money to do. So, you will get great, and sometimes rare, experiences.

Going to a sauna and having a dip in a pool outside in winter, as I have done on several occasions, might be exotic for you—but probably not so for us Finns. Before such an activity, we once drove a beach buggy on a ridiculously narrow, icy track. I still remember having a female colleague riding shotgun and shouting, "YOU ARE F******

CRAZY!" Well, I may have been going a bit fast, considering the circumstances.

Once, we went sailing on two 50-foot sail ships at the waters in the front of Helsinki. We had a little race against the other ship. It had to give up the chase, as its path was about to cross with one of the huge ferries coming from Sweden (the ferry had already started to sound its siren, as it cannot yield even to a sailing ship). I helped steer our ship, the S/Y Belmont (that once took part in a prestigious solo sailing competition around the world), back to its home harbor at night.

My driving skills came to a test also at Coala. We raced against each other in rally-converted Ford Sierras (with a stick shift and rear-wheel drive, obviously) on an only partly asphalted rallycross track. The experience included the traditional ceremonies at the podium, complete with the "champagne" one could spray around. Yes, Finns are a bit crazy about motorsports.

There are, of course, also many other ways of having fun with your colleagues. For example, some companies organize company-wide meetings with engaging performers and award ceremonies. Others participate in well-known diversity events.

In the end, it is you who will decide how much value you put on these kinds of events and activities (for example, singles probably value company parties more than married people, for obvious reasons). From some companies' point of view, they may be important selling points to get you to sign up, but many other aspects of the job should probably come first. There are even companies that offer less in terms of free events, food, and drinks—they may have chosen other ways to keep their employees happy. Also, remember that the world is changing, not the least because of the pandemic still ongoing at the time of writing. Some companies may decide to spend less money on events. At least, there are probably now restrictions on events that verge on overkill (such as crossing a country border in a project outing).

Does Being a Consultant Ruin Your Reputation?

Consulting does not really have an image issue as a profession. Consultants are generally respected as skilled professionals in their fields (of course, this can also depend on which company they work for). In the eyes of the average Joe, IT consultants can even have the advantage of working on something (more or less) concrete and not only flapping their tongue. But then again, there are countries (such as Finland) where many people believe that the state should minimize any differences in income. In that kind of culture, the average worker may not especially like anyone he or she thinks is earning more. There is even a word for this kind of attitude—jealousy.

Still, this has no negative consequences for the consultant in practice. In real life, I have seldom encountered any negative attitude against my profession. Usually, clients take me as an expert working for them. They treat me as a person (who would guess). A few of my friends have occasionally made fun of my profession, but that has been good-natured.

You may occasionally encounter a negative attitude against consultants at the client site. It has a lot to do whether the client has experience using consultants or not—and whether the experiences are positive or negative. Sometimes, the bad reputation is the consultants' own doing. And if using consultants is something new, there may be understandable suspicions among the client employees. For example, they may not like that the management hired consultants when there are (to their opinion) perfectly capable internal employees to do the job.

The attitude of a typical client employee also depends on what the consultants are tasked to do. There may be some (mild) hostility if the task is seen as something that will lead to negative consequences for the client employees (for example, reductions). The conclusions from the consultants' analyses may also be taken as personal critique by some. They will probably not say it to your face (although even that may happen), but rather speak behind your back and show a sour face.

I have encountered this kind of attitude in only a couple of client organizations. But you will for sure see it at some point. This is just something that consultants must be able to take. In addition to the client management speaking for you, there are no special tricks you can use to change the situation. Just continue to act courteously and deliver high quality. After all, the general attitude at the client site may change when the people get to know you.

Is It Only About Money?

Is consulting only about helping faceless corporations make more money and, naturally, making a lot of money while doing it? What about the meaning and impact of consulting? People want these things from their job, but it is, of course, not so simple.

Individuals find different things meaningful and appreciate different kinds of impact. Sometimes it is the work, sometimes the employer. Maybe you are just doing routine reports, but you are doing it for the Red Cross, right? Even if you are making your company's customers' lives easier by creating great solutions, it is just this limited number of people you are helping.

Whatever your criteria, you cannot deny that IT consultants have an impact on society. They build the IT solutions that keep things running in the public sector. They create new innovative solutions that transform organizations and even industries. And if you are looking for a personal impact, IT consultants make the lives of their client representatives easier. It is difficult *not* to find meaning in IT consulting.

Should You Really Change to IT Consulting?

You have your reasons for thinking about leaving your current job. Maybe your job is not challenging enough, or you cannot grow in your current position. Maybe you just want to try something different for a change. Or maybe your employment is fixed-term or temporary—and you *have* to find a new job. There can also be plenty of organizational reasons to drive the best employees away, from bad management to unwanted mergers and acquisitions.

You also have your reasons for wanting to change to IT consulting specifically. A career in IT consulting obviously has its advantages. I hope I have communicated some of them in this book, as well as some of the differences compared to internal employee positions. Remember that if you have the wrong expectations about consulting, becoming a consultant can be a bad move.

Before rushing to resign or applying to a new job, spend a moment to think about your reasons. You can start by making it clear to yourself what you want from work. You can use the examples in the section "Know Your Preferences" in the chapter "Know the Secrets of Landing Your Dream Job" to get some ideas.

Also, consider if a change to a different kind of career can really make your situation better. Changing to IT consulting does not necessarily solve your career problems. Especially if there is nothing badly wrong with your current job, you must consider if changing to consulting really makes sense. Let me be direct. Even if you think highly of yourself and are sure that you would make an excellent consultant, the job may still be too demanding or stressful for you.

You might be trading a comfortable job for one that requires you to constantly stretch yourself, deal with uncertainty, and even spend more time at work. Your pay may be only slightly better as a consultant. If you currently have excellent compensation, your salary as a consultant may even be lower. You might even lose your fancy manager title. In a consultancy, you need to *do* and not only give motivational speeches and delegate!

Is IT Consulting for Women?

Whoa, do not shoot me yet! Just keep on reading. I know that you would not believe anything a white youngish male would write on diversity matters. So, I asked a person who knows about these things—namely a woman working as an IT consultant. Let's hear her.

Before you begin reading, you should note that the author lives in Finland. Finland is a country currently governed by five women, some of which are quite young. It is also a country where the pronoun he/she does not distinguish gender. A country where hierarchies are low and respect of fancy titles is non-existent. As a result, these experiences might not be directly transferable to other countries.

IT is a new industry, at least compared to many others. A person may come from a long line of military service, but not from a long line of IT professionals. A fresh industry has room for new people, and everyone must prove their own worth. For the larger part of my working career, there have been less available professionals than open positions in the job market. It has been an employee's market. This has had its effects on the terms of labor, as well as benefits. Poor employee treatment is not advisable when everyone has two or three other options available for earning their daily bread.

Work in IT deals with concrete deliverables. It is at its simplest when coding software. Code from some people works well, and from others, not so well. It is also easy to recognize who is the most efficient coder. The respect of teammates comes from results, not fancy words or gender. The same applies to design work in IT. It is easy to see whose plan is good and feasible. Co-workers recognize quite quickly who really knows tech and who just talks about it.

A major part of IT consulting is about running projects. The project has a project manager who follows the progress. The project manager will defend his or her best people ferociously to complete the project. I have even seen a project manager fill travel expense applications for her best coder. Project members with weaker performance are eagerly traded off to other projects—even mid-project. And it also works similarly on the company level. Companies will take care of their best people to prevent them from leaving for competitors. However, in the largest organizations, the process for following performance might be somewhat broken, so this may be more of a lottery.

This type of performance and deliverable-based work tolerates the diversity of employees well. The factor that brings people together is professional know-how. In this line of work, you can dress as you like (as long as you are dressed). Your exterior habitus, gender, or any other factor is easily considered to have a very minor effect on your work. The most difficult conversations concern differences between programming languages, not politics. Sure, I have seen dividing lines in the workplace. But it just happens to be more of a division to "the no-nonsense people" and "what is that clown still doing here." Note that this has nothing to do with gender. A true geek could not care less for official diversity programs (regardless of gender). But sure, there should be procedures for dealing with sexual harassment, etc.

There are many companies in the industry that already have a very diverse workforce. They know that diversity is a competitive advantage and will make sure that new employees fit into this culture. But still, in many companies, the majority of the employees are men. So, as a woman, this has to be an okay setting for you. And when you step to a client site, you can encounter all kinds of opinions about gender roles—some of them extremely old-fashioned. You have to be able to take this as well (it is part of working in the service business).

Writing and presenting are precious skills for IT consultants. When writing specifications, the end result must be exact and legible. The contents are gathered by facilitating workshops, and the results need to be presented here and there. Women are typically strong in these areas. If you also have the ability for logical thinking (for example, math has always been your strong point), the chances of success are high. In most assignments, we do not deal with hardware anymore. I, myself, can install software on my own computer, but I will never play with it. You do not need to be enthusiastic about investigating your own laptop's technical details to design extensive information systems or to code. In large organizations, it is even forbidden to mess around with your computer.

To summarize, IT consulting is a nice well-paid job, especially for women. There are very diverse positions and roles in the field, so you will surely find something that fits your strengths and interests.

Do Seasoned Professionals Fit Into Consulting?

If you are one of the seasoned folks with over 20 years of work experience, you must approach your job search a bit differently. Age discrimination is a reality in many of today's workplaces. Whatever the excuses for it, I have the impression that it is even worse in the fast-paced IT consulting world. With all the money and effort large consultancies are throwing into their inclusion and diversity programs, the situation must get better eventually. But we are not there yet.

How can I, still in my thirties at the time of writing, advise you? I would first suggest revisiting your reasons for that career change. You already have the good compensation seniority often brings. Your job description is probably comfortable enough. Many consultancies cannot even match your current compensation. The problem is that, as my boss (a seasoned professional herself) says, your market value as an IT consultant is probably lower than your current compensation. If you get that consultant job, you will have to take on more challenging work for less money. Ask yourself, are the learning opportunities and other advantages of an IT consulting career worth it? And if you do not like it as a consultant, will you be able to get another job?

If you are, despite everything, still interested in a career in IT consulting, there are some good options for you. You can find a boutique consultancy whose specialization fits your profile well. Focus on companies whose owners are of similar age as you. These tend to be more seniority friendly. If you have an excellent network, starting your own company is a possibility. Also, consider getting into IT consulting *after* your pension age. If you are paid a pension, the risks of trying out your skills in IT consulting will be minimal.

Is IT Consulting Really for You?

By now, I have hopefully convinced you that IT consulting is a fine business. But is it really the right one for you? Some people just do not fit well in the consulting business. Some may fail miserably, while others may just be unhappy. And I do not mean the lack of technical skills. Those working in company internal IT expert positions may know the technical stuff related to their niche better than any consultant. But they may have very different attitudes and personality traits. These are difficult to change.

The requirements for a consultant are just different than those for IT experts. So, if you identify with any of the following traits and behaviors, you should take extra care in considering if the IT consulting business really is the right place for you.

- **If you are not willing to work hard**. If you play it right, it may be possible in some organizations to earn your living by being physically present, appearing busy, and hiring, eh, consultants to do your work. But the consulting business is not for the work-shy. You will *personally* need to create various high-quality deliverables efficiently and on schedule. And if you want to earn your fee by flapping your tongue, your advice needs to be extremely valuable—not a position you can get into easily. This does not mean that you necessarily must work extra-long days. You are just expected actually to work, hands-on—not only appear to work. Also, you will need to stretch yourself and take on new, challenging tasks. And always be willing and able to learn new things.
- **If you are not willing to take responsibility**. As a consultant, you need to take ownership of whatever you do. In consulting, everyone is expected to carry their weight. You just cannot hide behind your manager or teammates.
- **If you are reactive, not proactive**. Consultants need to drive forwards whatever they are working on. After all, that is one of the "superpowers" a good consultant has. They even get the client people moving. So, you cannot be passive and just wait for orders from your manager. It is, of course, fine

to ask for advice, but you must be active in seeking it. Still, there are cultural differences you must consider. In some cultures, you just *cannot* be proactive in certain positions.

- **If you cannot take uncertainty**. Let's get it straight. There is plenty of uncertainty in the IT consulting business. Only the ones who can adapt will make good consultants. In your day-to-day work at the client, you need to be prepared for surprises and putting out fires. If something major changes at the client's, the consultants are probably the last to know. Your client may even terminate your assignment. You may have to withstand long intervals on the bench and be able to take the hardships of looking for a new assignment.

- **If you do not want to work in a team**. Some people prefer to work solo for whatever reason. But for those about to begin a career in an IT consultancy, that preference does not go well. Except for the lone coaches and trainers, you will need to work as a team in IT consulting. You need to be able to work well with your colleagues, client employees, and even consultants from competing companies. The teams may be very diverse, with individuals from different cultures and with different backgrounds.

- **If you cannot handle critique**. As brought out, consultants must be able to handle negative attitude and undeserved critique from client employees. I know it is difficult to just sit there and smile when your client is acting passive-aggressive. But you must be able to do it. After all, consulting is like any service business. Consultants will get criticized easier than the client's own employees and probably get the worst of it if things get difficult. So, it will be stressful if you take things personally. Naturally, there will also be occasions when the critique is justified. You will not be a good employee *anywhere* if you cannot take feedback from your superiors, peers, and clients—and learn from it.

3. KNOW THE CONSULTING BUSINESS

Everything From Coding to Enterprise Architecture

Before beginning the search for your dream job, it is important to understand the big picture. Let me begin by sharing some stories of what kind of work I have done so far.

Fast Lane to Enterprise Architecture

The beginning of my career as an IT consultant was probably somewhat untypical. Unlike many, I did not at first work in an IT solutions development project. This is the work involving implementing, for example, a web portal for insurance customers, an enterprise resource planning system for a manufacturing firm, or some innovative mobile app. This is the work that people usually associate with IT consulting.

Instead, I was hired to the enterprise architecture business unit, which was closer to the management consulting type of work than the business lines doing mostly IT solution implementations. So, starting from my first project, I focused on advisory work. In these assignments, the client wants to have an answer to a complex question or a solution to a problem (or at least something that takes the client closer to having the solution). To put it simply, the work involves collecting information, analyzing it, and creating an architectural drawing or a report. For example, once we did a functional and technical analysis of the client's most critical IT solutions and gave the chief information officer (CIO) recommendations on what to do with them.

IT Solution Implementations Are the Bread and Butter

Sure, I have also been working in IT solution implementation projects. Also, in these, my work has had an architectural twist. I have created tons of solution architecture specifications that tell what the solution consists of and how it works. These are usually done by workshopping with the client on the needs and other things to be considered. This documentation is then used, among others, for deciding whether the solution should be actually implemented or not. Also, implementation teams use architecture documentation as a checklist to ensure that all the needs and dependencies have been considered.

Then there are the functional and technical analysis and design roles. I have been responsible for documenting detailed specifications for IT solutions. I have worked on requirements, use cases, user stories and designed integrations and configurations. This has involved many workshops and discussions with the client and meticulously familiarizing myself with the features and constraints of the technology to be used in each assignment. I have done this kind of work usually in a team of several consultants.

Enterprise Architecture Is My Business

I have worked most of my IT consulting career on enterprise architecture. It is not the architecture of a single IT solution but of the whole organization. Enterprise architecture takes a high-level view on the organization and its constituents, such as business services, processes, applications, and technology platforms. It also shows how the organization interacts with customers, partners, and authorities. It is a strategic management tool that describes what the organization has, what it can do, and what it wants to be in the future.

This kind of design has several uses. It provides a common vision of the future and valuable information for decision-making and solutions design. When you know what processes, information, and applications there are in the organization and how they are intertwined, you can make better decisions and create better plans. You need to know what you have before you can figure out how it should be improved, right?

In the enterprise architecture sphere, much of the work is about documenting the client's business and IT environments and creating designs on how it should be changed. This kind of work, of course, cannot be done alone. It involves many meetings, interviews, and workshops with different experts and leafing through masses of client documentation. The topic may sound fancy, but there are opportunities in enterprise architecture for both junior and senior consultants.

As this kind of architectural approach might be new to the client, starting with the basics usually works. In the cases where the customer is already doing something on enterprise architecture, I have spent time supporting the client in utilizing it in the best ways and providing appropriate methods and tools. I have used most of the tools of the trade and become an expert in them. Work on enterprise architecture has been highly satisfying, as you get to know the client's business and IT well. After some time doing it, you get to be an expert in your own right in the client's business.

There Is Much More Than Technical Work

Many people think IT consulting is about very technical work, such as coding and installing software. I have done very little of that in my career. My most technical work was probably a code review, which I did only once (in a development project, the coders submit their code to some other person to check for errors and other quality issues, such as insufficient commenting). I have also done functional testing on one occasion, but that is not so technical as it may sound. Testing is an important task, as it makes sure that the solution works as it should be. In practice, you follow a script and click things in the user interface, see if you get the right result, and report your findings.

A slightly more common technical task for me has been configuring packaged software to the client's needs. Once, I even created a proof-of-concept implementation of an identity and access management solution on the Azure platform using packaged software (identity and access management takes care that only the right individuals can access IT solutions and their data).

In another project, I configured dozens of access rights models to the identity and access management solution the client was using. That was probably the most factory-like consulting work I have ever done, lasting over a year and consisting of several sprints (development cycles)—all pretty similar. Still, we had a good team, and there was some client contact (with the application owners). We constantly improved our ways of working. While partly automating one phase of our work, I did the only real coding I have ever been paid to do, in Visual Basic.

IT consulting is far from being only technical work, such as coding and configuring software. Instead, it is a lot about working with people and understanding the business. Granted, there are also opportunities to dive into technology and seldom meet the client people, for those who enjoy working like that.

A Multitude of Assignments and Clients

The assignments I have worked on have been very differently organized. There have been the traditional IT solution projects of different sizes, managed and staffed by consultants. Then there have been the small advisory projects, where we have been hired to analyze the situation and create a plan of action or other documentation—management consulting style.

I have also worked as a resource at clients, under the management of the client. Once, I worked as an architect at a public sector client for three years, almost full time. I was close to being a client employee then—I was even invited to the parties. I have also worked in a project team consisting solely of consultants, almost all from different companies.

There have also been a variety of client organizations. I have seen different parts of the Finnish public sector and companies from different industries—anything from manufacturing to telecommunications to finance and insurance. There has also been a variety in size, from a little over a hundred employees to the largest in its industry (by Finnish standards, anyway). I have worked in high-visibility cases under CIOs' direct supervision and on the little (but absolutely necessary) technical details, only of interest to my own supervisor and a few experts from the client.

When you enter the field, the opportunities are pretty much limitless—if you choose your employer and position right. For my part, I am delighted and grateful for getting this huge variety of work, projects, and clients, in a little over ten years of IT consulting. You only get this kind of variety if you work as a consultant.

But let's dive right into the world of IT consulting and see what it really is—and what it is not.

What Is Consulting?

First, let's see what consulting is all about. We will look at, for example, what consulting is, why anyone would hire a consultant, and what kind of consultants there are. We will also take a closer look at the ultimate goal of consulting—creating value for the client.

The Basics

Consulting is about providing expertise for clients for a fee. The clients are organizations that need someone to do a job they do not want to or lack the skills, resources, or time, to do for themselves. The consultants then do whatever the client requires, be it giving advice, solving problems, or creating new IT solutions.

A typical consulting engagement is a one-off endeavor, called a *project*. A consultant may also work for the client as a *resource* in a permanent fashion (well, as permanent as it gets in consulting), doing his or her work almost like a client employee. Consulting can also be about providing continuous service for the client. Even whole business processes can be outsourced to a consulting company.

Consultants work in different kinds of companies. There is a large variety there, ranging from a several hundred thousand employee multinational to a local single person IT consulting startup. Also consulting clients are diverse organizations ranging from Fortune 500 companies to the public sector and even startups. Depending on the specifics of the engagement, the consultants may work at the client site, at their own office, or at home. Some may be traveling a lot, but that is not something every consultant has to do.

Why hire consultants and not new employees? Generally, consultants can be hired faster than employees. Where else would you get a ten-person team to develop a new mobile app on a few week's notice? And if the need is only temporary, it is not even a good idea to hire a new employee. Good consultants are also experts in their fields, so hiring a consultant is a good way to get the skills and knowledge needed for the job. Also, consultants bring an external viewpoint to the issue at hand, which can be crucial for solving it. They also bring experience on how things have been done in other organizations—and what worked there and what did not. Senior management may also hire consultants to do organizationally difficult things, such as planning major changes or suggesting ways to cut costs.

Hiring a consultant also gives a good guarantee that the person can actually assign time for the project. That may not be true for the employees in today's organizations, who have many responsibilities. And finally, consultants are typically driven people who make sure that the task is finished. This can act as a necessary kick in the butt for the client employees. All things considered, hiring a consultant can get the job done faster and may even be cheaper than hiring an employee.

In principle, anyone who has expertise that someone is willing to pay for can be a consultant. So, there are consultants and consultants. Those who have the skills, experience, and knowledge to help their clients can become trusted advisors and extremely valuable for their clients. However, not every consultant does something valuable. A consultant can also be totally useless or even harmful. Consequently, a consultant needs something to distinguish oneself from the mass and get the client to trust that he or she is the right one for the job. This also has a lot to do with selling. A consultant (even if not engaged in sales as it is usually understood) has to sell himself or herself to the client every day by their work.

Different Consultants

There are, of course, many kinds of expertise. Therefore, consultants can be specialized in different fields. These specializations can be broad or narrow. Some consultants are generalists, that can do many types of work. The broadest distinction is between management consultants and IT (or technology) consultants, but there are also other kinds of consultants. For example, there are consultants specialized in improving a specific corporate function, such as finance, marketing, sales, operations, or HR. Also, there are consultants in the field of construction but do not ask me what they do.

Management consultants (also called strategy or business consultants) are specialized in solving various business challenges. Their work can involve, for example, creating a new strategy, planning mergers and acquisitions, and streamlining operations. If you are interested in this kind of consulting, *The McKinsey Way* by Ethan Rasiel is an excellent read on the topic.

IT consulting is an umbrella term covering a large amount of different work related to technology. It is, of course, sometimes difficult to distinguish it from management consulting. Even though the assignments may have different goals, the methodology used can be very similar. For example, both IT and management consultants may run workshops, analyze the client situation, formulate suggestions, and deliver the resulting report to the client.

Implementing an IT solution may be an obvious example of an IT consulting assignment. Still, it is far from being the only type of work in the field. There are also very business-oriented and strategic IT consulting assignments, such as planning IT strategies, designing services, and improving processes. On the other hand, there are also technology-oriented management consulting assignments.

Still, for a consultant working in the field, the distinction is often clear. In large consultancies, IT and management consulting are usually separate business lines, with different work cultures. Smaller consultancies, on the other hand, are often specialized in one specific type of consulting. Consultants may have different backgrounds, either in business or IT. Still, a person's background does not necessarily restrict one to a particular type of consulting.

Value Is the Key

Consulting is a service business. Even though clients (and the ones who pay the bill) are almost always organizations, the actual customers are the people working at the client. These individuals must perceive that they are getting value from the consultant's work. Of course, there are many ways to create value. Some consultants analyze a company's situation or problem and give recommendations on how to proceed. Some give motivational speeches. Some coach individuals. And some, like the IT consultants this book is about, often create different deliverables for the client.

A *deliverable* is consultant-speak for anything the consultants are hired to make to create value for the client. They range from working IT solutions to different documentation, such as reports and architectural models—that can then be used as a basis for other work. Of course, creating the deliverable should not be an end in itself. Meeting the client's expectations and creating value is rather the key.

Consulting is both an art and a science. Even though the solutions consultants create are based on proven methods and technologies, logical reasoning, and solid calculations, they also need to look great. It is not enough that the solutions do something useful. So, this is also a creative profession. Even if you follow good practices, there is a lot left for the individual consultant's creativity.

Consulting is interaction and communication. A textbook example of a consultant is someone with excellent presentation and influencing skills. Granted, there are people in the field who can save a doomed assignment by turning substandard deliverables into gold, by using only their gift of speech. But this is not a skill IT consulting is usually about. In everyday work, other communication skills come to use. You must be able to gather information through interviews and workshops. You must be able to work effectively with others. You must write clearly. You must *listen* and be able to understand what you heard or read. You have to assimilate vast amounts of information, tell what is important, and summarize it into a deliverable.

Whether you are an extrovert or introvert (or anything in between), you can become a great consultant. Everything you do must translate to money in your company's bank account, usually in the form of billing. And someone must do the real work to be billed. So, there are plenty of opportunities for individuals who like to *do* rather than only talk about it.

Types of IT Consulting Assignments

IT consulting assignments come in different flavors. The type of engagement defines how the work is organized and what its terms are. Here are the types of consulting assignments you will most often encounter.

Consulting Project

These assignments are the ones you will most probably work on when you are employed in a medium-sized or large IT consultancy. The consulting work is carried out in a project set up and managed by the consulting company. The consultancy staffs the project team with *resources* (consultant jargon for project members) that fill the *roles* required for the job. A role in this context means the category of work a consultant does in a client engagement (such as a developer, a designer, a tester, or a solutions architect). You may be staffed to more than one project if required but working in a large project is usually a full-time job.

If you are a junior employee or the project is large, you probably do not have to do anything to initiate or manage the project. You just start working in your role, and the project manager or your team lead will tell you what to do. The project manager and the senior consultants in key roles do the project planning. The project manager is responsible for running the project.

The largest enterprise system implementations may involve several projects, each staffed by dozens of consultants, may take years to finish, and cost a significant percentage of the client's annual IT budget. On the other hand, projects for advisory work may be staffed with only one or two consultants and be finished in a few weeks or months.

Working as a Resource

This means that you are working for the client without having a project managed by your company. If you are employed by a very small firm, this is how you will probably work (the other option is a tiny consulting project). The client hires you to do a particular kind of work, such as being a solutions architect or a tester. The role can be full-time or part-time.

Your work can even be close to what the client's employees working in similar roles do. This may be similar to being employed by the client—except that you are probably paid better than the average client person and can avoid a lot of organizational chaff the client employees have to take.

Your supervisor can be a particular employee (usually a manager) from the client or another consultant hired by the client. In terms of your own company, you are on your own. Still, there is probably some person from your company you can go to for support. There may even be multiple persons from your company working at the same client as resources.

Consultants working as resources can work in the client's own projects. The client can even staff them entirely with consultants. I once worked in a ten-person team where everyone (except two) was employed by a different consulting firm! On another occasion, I was working for years with a colleague in an architect role at a client, under the client's chief architect's direction.

Continuous Service

Continuous services are basically positions or tasks that the client outsources to the consulting company. These can range, for example, from maintaining an IT solution to providing an outsourced product owner or IT security team. In this kind of job, your boss is at the consultancy. If providing the service is not a full-time job, you must work for multiple clients. Typically, large and medium-sized companies have continuous services in their catalog.

What Kinds of Work Do IT Consultants Do?

Basically, there are the assignments about implementing a particular IT solution and the ones that are not. In addition to these, IT consultants may do some work for their *own* company. Consultants can also be between assignments. Let's take a closer look at these.

IT Solution Implementations

Implementing an IT solution is the typical IT consulting project. By an IT solution, I mean a set of software (and the hardware it runs on) used for a certain purpose. The terms *system* and *application* are also used in the field and are pretty close. By *implementation*, I mean all the steps required to take an IT solution into use.

There are many different types of solutions, ranging from simple mobile applications to extensive enterprise systems the client cannot function without. There are solutions that the users directly interact with. Then, some solutions provide functionalities to support other solutions (these include, for example, identity and access management, integration, and shared data storage solutions).

For example, I have been involved with designing enterprise systems such as enterprise resource planning and customer relationship management for public sector clients. Then, there were several custom-built solutions for particular needs. There have also been a couple of projects on implementing a web portal, for example one that allows corporate customers to manage their insurance policies.

The project does not have to be about creating a completely new IT solution, which is coded from scratch for the client. It can also be about implementing some ready-made software product. These only need to be installed and configured to be usable. It can also be about doing an overhaul for an older IT solution or integrating several solutions so that they can work together.

There is a multitude of roles IT consultants can work in. If you are the project manager, you are responsible for the whole project. If you are an architect, you will draw models that tell how the solution works and what it consists of. If you work as an analyst or designer, you will document, for example, how the users use the solution, what the user interface looks like, and how data is used within the solution. If you are a developer, you are responsible for actually building the solution. And finally, as a tester, you will test that the solution works as it should be after it has been put together.

This is not a complete list but probably has the most typical roles. In some cases, you can hold several roles. For example, the project team members may take turns to do architecting, design, developing, and testing especially in agile development. Naturally, this is something for only experienced IT consultants.

Advisory Work

Not all IT consulting work is about implementing IT solutions. *Advisory work* is the umbrella term I will use for this kind of IT consulting in this book because a major part of this work *is* about giving advice. Of course, it encompasses many different kinds of consulting assignments. Let's take a look at the most typical examples.

There are those assignments where the client requests an investigation into something, a plan of action, enterprise architecture content, or other documentation. This kind of work results in deliverables such as reports, plans, instructions, and architectural models. These assignments are often done as small projects but may also be some of the tasks of an IT consultant working as a resource.

Basically, you talk to people, go through piles of documentation, do some analysis and summarizing, recycle some of your own and your colleagues' old slides, and put together a convincing document, usually a PowerPoint presentation. The outcome is then (hopefully) used by the client in follow-up work. It may also lead to another consulting assignment for the same or a different consultancy.

Some real examples of this kind of work include creating an overview of the IT solutions used in different parts of the business, designing architectural guidelines for carrying out a major IT overhaul, and collecting basic information on the client's IT solutions. Surprisingly, many organizations do not have an overview of the systems and applications they are using.

IT consultants can also be hired to improve and implement methodologies and tools. These are used in, for example, managing IT services, running projects, developing IT solutions—and modeling and utilizing enterprise architecture. You will create instructions, process descriptions, and user guides. You will also have to do training, coaching, and even motivational speaking to get people to work in new ways. The work is often a project, but ongoing support can also be provided by consultants working at the client as resources, or as part of a continuous service.

The most senior IT consultants may act as coaches, usually to senior client employees. You will, for example, have discussions, answer questions, observe the client in work situations, and give appropriate exercises and feedback. These help the client to improve his or her ways of working.

On the Bench

It is not an assignment, but everyone will probably be on it at some point. Being on the bench means not be staffed in a client assignment. Consultants on the bench can be between assignments or waiting for their first project. It is common to be on the bench for at least a few days while waiting for the next assignment. It only becomes a problem if you are on the bench for an extended period, say a few weeks or a month. As an employee, you are still paid a salary even if you are not working for a client (however, depending on your pay model, you may be paid less than when you are billing all your work time).

If you are on the bench, you are sometimes given something meaningful to do. See the next section for some examples. While I have heard rumors of some consultants using bench time for watching Netflix all day long, it is one of the rare occasions you actually have time for anything else than client work. Therefore, the time should be used well. Suitable activities while on the bench include studying, attending seminars and other work-related events, updating your consultant CV, blogging (work-related, of course), networking, and any kind of internal work. If you have an exhausting assignment behind you, it also pays to recharge your batteries a bit.

Internal Work

There are dedicated people in medium-sized and large consultancies to take care of other aspects of the business than the consulting part. They do, for example, sales, marketing, HR, finance, and even IT. Consultants are needed to support some of these tasks. In small consultancies, most of them fall to the consultants themselves. I call this *internal work* as it is not billable from clients.

A typical internal task any IT consultant will do at some point of his or her career, is sales support. The dedicated salespeople cannot know the specifics of the subject matter. They need help from consultants to make a convincing offer with profitable pricing. Typically, consultants are asked to define the necessary tasks and provide realistic work and cost estimates. In practice, the support may be anything from brainstorming with sales reps to writing a few paragraphs of text to an offer. In small firms, consultants need to do everything sales-related themselves.

Content marketing is another typical example. This means presenting, posting, or otherwise sharing content related to your (and your company's) expertise. The point is to give something useful to potential customers (for free) and show that you and your company have the relevant expertise—without directly saying "buy from us." So, you might present in various events, post to LinkedIn, or write a blog on your company's website, for example. In small companies, you will probably have more freedom to use your creativity. In contrast, in larger ones, you will most likely just share your company's official marketing message.

There are, of course, many other internal tasks a consultant without (or with) chargeable work may be put to. For example, there may be internal documentation to update, internal training to give, or even product and service development to do.

Whatever You Do, Do Not Forget Billing

After providing value for the client, billing is the second most important task of a consultant. Consulting companies live and die of the work billed from their clients. *Chargeability* (the percentage of work time that can be billed from clients) is one of the most important metrics for a consultant.

Before the engagement begins, the consulting company and the client agree on the terms, including prices and billing. Typically, the consulting company handles the billing for the individual consultants. Often consultants charge by the hour or the day, but the fee can also be per project. For continuous services, there is a service fee.

The takeaway for the IT consultant is to always report the information needed for billing on time. Consulting firms usually have an application where consultants log their work. Sometimes just logging one's work in time is all that is required for billing—but not always. So, follow the guidelines and deadlines for time reporting set by your project manager.

Where Do the Assignments Come From?

There are many ways a consultancy can get a new assignment. If the consultancy is well-known and respected in its field, there is probably no need for selling as it is usually understood. The clients will come to the consultancy with their needs. It also pays to sell to current clients. If a consultancy is already delivering something for the client, setting up an extension or a new assignment can sometimes be done with less bureaucracy.

In less fortunate circumstances, the consultancy must actively search for clients. For example, seminars and industry associations are important forums for this kind of networking. Some approach potential clients by email. Some even do cold calling (but probably not very successfully).

Especially in smaller consultancies, a lot of work may come through subcontracting. This means that a consultancy or a broker gives another consultancy a call and asks if they could spare a resource or two for their assignment. The firm that owns the assignment then gets a certain commission from the subcontractor (for example, a percentage of the consultant's hourly fee). Everybody wins.

After getting the client-to-be around the same table for discussion, the consultants try to understand the client's needs. The client may then request an offer. This document describes what the consultants will do, how it benefits the client, and the terms (for example, pricing). Contributing to an offer is the type of sales support work IT consultants usually take part in. After accepting the offer, the consultancy and the client may also sign a formal contract.

Then there are public tenders, where the process is a bit different. These are opportunities for selling work and/or products published by public sector organizations. Companies then submit offers that are put to compete against each other. The one that gets the most points by predefined criteria wins the contract.

From what I have seen of public tenders in Finland, the criteria naturally favor low price. There may also be a set of somewhat strange or far-fetched quality characteristics. The bidding process is extremely formal. Sometimes the price is also too low to be profitable for the consultancy. Still, there are some good, long term opportunities available by public tender. By the way, if you are asked to provide your consultant CV for one of these, follow the instructions to the letter.

What does this then mean for a new IT consultant? In most cases, you do not have to find yourself an assignment. Others will do the necessary sales work. You will be just staffed in an assignment and start working. Even if you work in a small consultancy, it is usually not your *personal* responsibility to find new clients and assignments. Naturally, you will need to contribute to sales cases (as described above). Still, you will not have the sole responsibility of them. This is one of the main advantages of working as an employee as opposed to an entrepreneur.

Can Your Title Be Master of the Universe?

Some people are crazy about fancy titles and the status that comes with them. In some cultures, you will even *need* a fancy title to be taken seriously. A title can also be given as a reward for a job well done. For some, it is even more important than compensation. For others, their title may be almost meaningless. In any case, you cannot brush titles aside in IT consulting.

In large consulting firms, titles come standardized. These companies have predefined career paths that consist of career levels. As you get promoted, you gain a level. Each level comes with a matching title and a new set of expectations. For example, junior consultants may be called analysts. Consultant is a title for ones with a couple of years' experience under their belts. Those with project management responsibilities can be titled managers, managing consultants, or lead consultants. There are more glorified titles for those at the very top.

Some young and innovative consultancies may allow you to select your own title (within reason). Also, in tiny companies, you *could* have whatever title you wanted. Still, you should be conservative about it. In the best case, a potential client might find an overly glorified title amusing. For example, it can be hard to take someone titled chief technology officer seriously if they come from a company with two employees. It is also somewhat funny to be called managing consultant if there is no one working under you.

In the worst case, your selection of title will lose you business. For example, if you are being sold to a client to work in an expert role, your title should tell your client that you actually *do*, not just manage. Your title should be similar to the titles of client employees doing the same kind of work. For the same reason, you should not use titles like CEO or chairman of the board when working in a client assignment—even if you have such a title in your company. Still, consider adding owner or partner in your title if you own shares of your non-listed consultancy (this means a company whose shares are not publicly traded through a stock exchange). It tells you are particularly committed.

That is why an IT consultant can have many titles. There is the title you have as an employee of a consultancy. This is your "official" title. It can be printed on your business card. You may also have a different title that describes the role you are currently working in. That title can be put on offers, and you can use it when working at the client. For example, my official title is senior consultant & partner. That is not inconsistent with what I do for clients. Still, it often serves no purpose to highlight that I am a consultant while on an assignment, especially if I am working as a resource. Therefore, in offers, I am often introduced as an enterprise architect. I might also put that on my client email signature. Naturally, my CV has the official title. To avoid any misunderstanding, I also tell client representatives that I am a consultant when I meet them for the first time.

4. KNOW THE COMPANIES

From the Giant to the Boutique

Before applying to any IT consulting job, you should know what kind of company makes the best employer for you. Different types of companies suit different individuals. For example, you should consider your work experience, career goals, work style, and personality when deciding which company is the right one for you.

Here, I present a categorization of IT consulting companies, which brings out many of their characteristics. This will help you in deciding which type of companies would be the best fit for you. So, let's dive into the topic by comparing the companies in my career journey, the global consulting giant and Coala. This familiarizes you with many of the characteristics you should consider when thinking about your preferences for an employer.

Consulting firms are numerous, and they come in different types and sizes. Large, multinational consulting companies have hundreds of thousands of employees worldwide. These consulting giants are prestigious and well-established. They have set procedures and instructions for everything—from working in a particular role to having development discussions.

When I joined one of these companies, they immediately put me through a week-long onboarding period that made the start of my IT consulting career smooth. I was assigned a *career counselor* who is basically a senior consultant who acts as your coach and supervisor in development discussions (I still keep in contact with him). Before my first project, I attended a two-week core consulting course in the US. They taught everything a new consultant needs to know, from the IT solution lifecycle to interviewing clients and creating deliverables. This time was also socially memorable (remember I met my partner there). And no, at least this company does not send you to a training course across the Atlantic anymore. Well, it was fun while it lasted.

Generally, large companies have large projects. Even though enterprise architecture projects tended to be rather small in terms of the project team's size, IT solution implementation projects were larger. So, I usually worked either with one or two more senior consultants or just as a member of a team with ten or more people. And as brought out in the previous chapter, I did various work related and not related to IT solution implementation. There was probably a project about every major type of enterprise system.

Almost all my work time was chargeable work, but I also worked in a support role in a couple of sales cases. Usually, I was working for only one client at a time. Even though there was freedom in how to carry out my own work, I felt I was only one small cog in the machine. I felt I could not make a noticeable impact on the company.

Joining Coala was totally different. I was the first employee to join the company, besides the two entrepreneur-owners. There was not much in terms of onboarding, but at least I already had five years of consulting experience. The company was founded just two years before I joined, but it already had long-term clients—so work was steady. I got into a client assignment immediately.

I was the main, and sole, person from our company working at the client. That was the first huge difference. I could tap into the knowledge of my manager, but I was mostly on my own. Following this, I have been either the only person from my company working at the client's, or a pair to another consultant. Larger consulting teams have been scarce, and in every case, they have involved consultants from other companies. I have usually worked for multiple clients at the same time. Billing five different clients in a month is my record, but the typical number is closer to two.

When it comes to sales support and other internal work, the situation was also totally different. In a small company, everyone must contribute to sales. I have worked on numerous offers, attended many sales meetings, and demoed architecture modeling tools to potential clients. Later, I developed an interest and aptitude for content marketing.

Nowadays, I do an open webinar every two to three months, post and comment actively on LinkedIn, and present in industry events.

My role has changed a great deal over the years. I have grown to be a key employee for the firm, which is a position extremely difficult to get in when working in a larger consultancy. There is also much flexibility in making the job more and more like me. You can see this freedom also in small things. Heck, I can even choose the brand of coffee for the office (usually organic dark roast).

There are, of course, also many other kinds of IT consulting companies. I have experienced pretty much the extremes, but in the middle, there are many potential employers. Grouping these is a huge simplification. The companies have diverse roots, focus on different kinds of work, technologies, and clients—and are also very different as employers. And then there are the freest IT consultants of them all, the self-employed. Some consultancies probably do not even fit into my categorization. These may include, for example, large Indian IT consultancies—that I know very little about.

Let's take a closer look at what kind of IT consulting companies there are and what kind of employers they make. I have also attempted to bring out their characteristics to help you pick the right sort for you.

The Consulting Titans

In addition to the Big Three (they also do IT consulting), the Consulting Titans include all the other large, global, and well-known consulting companies such as Accenture, Capgemini, Deloitte, EY, KPMG, and PwC. These are the companies that you will find in listings labeled "Top Consulting Companies" and such on the internet. While the largest have over a hundred thousand employees globally, any global consulting company with several thousands of employees falls into this category.

These companies are generally respected as both consulting service providers and employers. They are here to stay and will have work in good and bad economic times. They include pure consulting companies and consulting departments of accounting firms. Some of them have only later extended into IT consulting. While they all have their nuances, you can find many commonalities. The characteristics may be similar, but different companies have different combinations of them.

The companies provide a wide variety of services. So, there are a lot of different kinds of projects. At their best, these companies give their employees great visibility to the different kinds of work done in IT consulting. Smaller companies cannot even offer the extensive IT solutions implementation projects as these giants can. You will also meet many people with a wide range of expertise. However, sometimes consultants may get stuck in the same large project for years against their will. This may limit them from getting some of the benefits of a consulting career, especially variety in work and clients. It may also limit their career progress.

There is a policy or standardized process for everything in these firms, so there is less space for doing things your way or having a say in things. You are merely a resource row in Excel and are staffed according to your employer's needs and preferences, not yours. You will, for sure, encounter some red tape. There is a jumble of different committees and initiatives whose impact on employees' personal growth and job satisfaction can sometimes be questionable.

Also, career progression comes standardized. Traditionally, these companies have forced everyone through the same career path—that of a generalist managing consultant, who is also competent in sales. If you fit that form, you may do very well. Still, times are changing. Now, in some companies, there are meaningful options for people more inclined to be experts and those who want to specialize in a specific client industry, type of IT solution, or technology.

Expectations are extremely high for those who are farther in their careers. They may end up responsible for a large project, a program, or a client. The most senior employees are even expected to open new areas of business. In some companies, it is "up or out": constant career progress is strongly encouraged, and those not able to do so are suggested to seek new challenges elsewhere. Still, the ones at the lower career levels are given more slack.

In some of these companies, competition can be fierce as consultants are ranked against their peers. Even though people are generally intelligent and friendly, competitiveness can harm teamwork. Excellent political skills and perhaps a certain amount of ruthlessness is required to advance to the few highest positions. The compensation for the most senior employees is excellent. Still, you must also consider what you have to give up for it.

These companies are an excellent choice for those beginning their IT consulting careers. They provide you with standardized onboarding and training. A large project makes a relatively safe environment for learning. You also get coaching, templates, and methodologies to get you up to speed. Working for a well-known and respected company is also great for your CV or resume. You gain credibility with clients by merely being employed in such a firm. The flip side is that these companies also use their brand to get new employees. In some companies and geographies, those fresh out from university may be surprised by the rather low starting salary. As everything is standardized, you probably cannot even negotiate a better deal.

These firms are also known for their parties, communal events, and free-time activities. Christmas, winter, and summer parties go without saying and are well organized. There are also clubs (with company funding) for different hobbies and interests. My employer's specialty was an annual skiing trip to a resort in Eastern Finland, on a chartered train. For the better or worse, you will feel yourself being part of the community.

The Mid-Sized Motley Group

These companies are a varied bunch. Some cover the whole spectrum of IT consulting. Some are specialized in different technologies, industries, or types of work—be it agile software development, IT management, strategic IT consulting, or tool consulting. There may even be hundreds or thousands of these firms in your country. Some of them are global, but most operate locally or in a few countries. The number of employees can vary from hundreds to a thousand or so (although there are some larger companies that belong to this group rather than to the Consulting Titans).

Their roots are diverse. Some have been born as boutique consultancies or even one-person startups and then grown organically or by acquiring other companies. There are IT service companies that do not confess to being consultancies. Then there are software and hardware vendors that want to be IT consultancies and such companies where consulting is still only a small part of the overall business. There are ones with a very narrow specialization, such as a particular brand of a software product.

You will see great diversity in business models, organization structures, and cultures. A colleague provided a handy categorization for these companies. The first group consists of modern, agile, and innovative firms. The second group includes companies that want to be in the Consulting Titans category—but are worse in every respect.

Companies in the first group tend to be cool, popular, and generally known as excellent employers. They do not necessarily even want to grow to be new Consulting Titans.

On the other hand, companies in the second group include old-fashioned computer companies, bureaucratic matrix organizations, and makers of half-hearted software products. For the employee, they might be, in the best case, nothing special. But they can also be worse. The avid jobseeker should note these differences and carefully consider where to apply. It is important to know one's preferences. You should use the advice in the next chapter to filter the cool from the colorless.

Generally, an IT consultant's life in these companies is more laid back than in the Consulting Titans. There is more freedom overall and room for negotiating your terms of employment. There is still the feeling of a smaller firm, and the community is tighter than in the larger firms. Fewer people means you get to know them better. You might even end up in the same elevator with the CEO. Depending on the organization, the workforce may be more or less heterogeneous.

These companies are generally economically weaker than their larger counterparts. Therefore, reductions can be expected in bad times. Also, expect restructuring and mergers & acquisitions in the future. While these can present a career opportunity, you will also end up in a different kind of company than you signed up for.

Some companies have a flat organization which gives more responsibility to individual employees. Those interested in internal work may also find plenty of opportunities. And if you have expertise that is highly valuable for a particular company, you will get compensated well. The better employers also offer extra benefits and a variety of free-time activities.

The Niche Players

These are boutique consultancies that are highly specialized and well-known in their own niches. The specializations vary from specific types of work (such as enterprise architecture or identity and access management) to a particular software product, tool, or methodology. Consequently, the assignments and roles available are less varied. Employees tend to have similar expertise. Size-wise, these companies vary from very small to a few hundred employees. Most of them are local, but some have an international dimension.

For those willing to specialize and grow themselves as an expert, boutique consultancies are an excellent choice. You can work on what you most like and are interested in. In small consultancies, career progress is a two-edged sword, though. You can always get to be a better expert, but there are seldom opportunities to grow yourself as a manager. There just are no positions available to progress to. And if fancy titles are important for you, these companies are probably not for you.

On the other hand, there is constant interaction with the owner-managers, lots of client contact, and great visibility for your work. You can also freely define your own job within limits set by your assignments. This also comes with responsibility, as no one will actively supervise you. You are responsible for your own continued education and getting help when you need it. There might be very few communal activities. In some cases, you may feel like a lone, self-employed consultant. Some of these firms are consulting brokers that do little more than offer their employees client assignments and handle the billing. If you like working independently, these firms may be the only places (besides having your own consulting firm) where you can find such a position in the industry.

In a small firm, everyone does pretty much everything. Expect to handle some of the office routines yourself, as there might not be dedicated staff for that. Everyone can also be asked to do selling and marketing (according to their abilities). This also brings great opportunities if you are interested in internal work. There is freedom and room to innovate. If you are eager and have what it takes, the opportunities are pretty much limitless.

Working at a niche player is usually not for fresh graduates. Of course, these companies can have both junior and senior people. Still, usually they are looking for employees with some work experience. As you may be the sole person responsible for an assignment, expectations are high. This does not mean that you must work crazy hours. You just have to carry more weight than your counterpart in a twenty-person project. You may also have to take multiple client assignments if one is not enough to fill your days.

When choosing a boutique consultancy employer, it is crucial to consider the people already working there. You will be meeting them regularly, so it is important to be comfortable with them. Risk and uncertainty are also considerations. These companies do not have a large cash reserve, so a few months of no business might mean the end for them. Employees not able to carry their weight are also readily shown the door.

Even with these risks, the pay may not be great, especially for those with less experience. But if you find the right niche for you, you can get along comfortably. The few best employees may be offered a partnership in the firm. A way to reward and motivate employees known from prestigious law firms, it means that you are permitted to buy a small share of the company. This brings an opportunity to benefit financially through getting paid dividends or if your firm is acquired. Still, it may come with new responsibilities (that is, more work). In fact, partnerships may also be offered by larger non-listed consultancies, but it is more probable to get to be a partner in a smaller company.

If you do not seem to have luck applying to large consultancies, it is worth considering a small one. A small and obscure (for potential employees, anyway) consultancy does not get so many applications. So, your application may be considered more thoroughly. Even if they cannot hire you at that moment, it is worth the try. This is a little-known opportunity, especially for seasoned professionals.

The Self-Employed

Many consultants have found working in a one-person firm to suit them well. Usually, these individuals are specialized in their own technological or methodological niche. For example, some manage projects, some create architecture, and some do coding. The company can be a startup or one with a long history. There may be growth targets, or there may not. Eventually, the company can grow in terms of headcount. Some entrepreneurs prefer being the sole employee and do not wish to hire more people, ever.

Individuals working in these firms are responsible for everything that is needed to run the business, including sales and marketing. Of course, they can outsource routine tasks such as bookkeeping and web design. There is much freedom, but also a lot of hard work. It is crucial to have excellent networks to find new work. You also need plenty of consulting experience and a great CV. Still, it is not granted that you find enough work all the time. And if you do not get work, you will not get paid. So, at least in the beginning, you cannot be too choosy and may need to take on less attractive (and less lucrative) assignments. For a new and unknown consultancy, being a subcontractor to a larger firm may be the only option.

I know several people who successfully employ themselves as IT consultants and love it for the freedom it provides. When you are your own boss, there are no other takers for your company's income (except, of course, the national tax authority). Still, few self-employed IT consultants make it big and are paid top dollar for their services—but you can get enough to live very comfortably. You can also choose how much you want to earn and work only that much.

Still, this option is not for the inexperienced or those not willing to work hard. As a self-employed consultant put it:

"it is a rocky road even with the 15 years of IT consulting experience under my belt." According to statistics, nine out of ten startups fail (although not immediately), so there is a big risk involved.

Entrepreneurship and startups are pretty popular topics, and you will find plenty of literature along these lines. Still, I would not recommend it for those at the beginning of their consulting careers. A safer option is to gain experience as an employee in a larger firm. You will gain valuable work experience, grow your network, and see what kind of work you like. After a few years in a reputable consulting company's service, the leap to your own consulting startup is smaller.

5. KNOW THE SECRETS OF LANDING YOUR DREAM JOB

Many Ways to Get a Job

Before getting started in your job search, I would like to share some of my own experiences from my work history. As you will learn, there are several ways to get yourself a position in IT consulting.

To My First IT Consulting Job

One early winter morning back in 2008, I was on the road earlier than usual, driving through the swirling snow. The highway to Helsinki was, for the most part, dark and slippery despite the regulation winter tires. It was a three-hour trip by car from where I lived at the time, and I was trying hard to keep it safe, by the rules, and on schedule. After parking in a hypermarket garage, I still had about twenty minutes to cover the last few hundred meters by foot.

I had applied to a position at a large, global consulting company and been invited to an interview. A few months later, I would be driving the same way, that time with my station wagon crammed with the essentials for a move to a new city. Applying to this company was a typical case of applying for a job. I had checked for open positions and found a perfect one—Enterprise Architecture Consultant. I filled an application on the web, added a cover letter and my CV.

I was first interviewed by an HR representative on my general aptitude and then by my potential supervisor about the subject matter. We munched on biscuits and sipped coffee (my supervisor-to-be had that for lunch, but I did not take that as a warning). It was all very pleasant. The only challenge thrown in was being asked to present a framework related to my present job on a flipboard in English. I was offered the job a few days after.

Sounds easy, but in this case, it probably helped enormously to have the right background. There could not have been many people among the applicants who could say they had experience in enterprise architecture. Mine was from academic research, but all the same. I knew the basics of the subject matter and had learned some useful skills when doing research at the university. Interviewing, facilitating focus groups, presenting, managing a project, and analyzing and summarizing information are obviously valuable skills also in consulting.

Change to a Boutique Consultancy

Getting a job at Coala at end-year 2012 was a different experience. I had met a person I had worked for at a former client at a get-together. Afterward, we had a chat over a beer. I had a gut feeling that something could come from that, and it did. A few days after, the person called me and asked if I would be interested in working at Coala, an architecture consultancy founded less than two years before. Sometime after an informal interview over plastic-wrapped muffins and carbonated water, I was offered the job.

Getting the job was pretty effortless, but again, I had just the expertise needed for the position. And even more importantly, I had left a good impression when working together for several months with the recruiter—now Coala's CEO. He even told me later that I was one of the best potential employees he had ever met. So, do your best in every client engagement. Your former client representatives will remember it.

My University Job and Earlier

Applying for my university job in December 2005, a few months before getting my master's, is a story on its own. It involves attending a surprise job interview being hungover after a night out with my friends, having just arrived home for the Christmas holidays from a student exchange in the UK. Suffice to say; it was the first hit after sending out dozens of applications—mostly ones for internal IT positions in various companies.

Back then, I did not know IT consulting was a possibility. Yes, searching for a job is strenuous, and I was tired of it. I had had no better luck before applying for a summer job in IT. The only jobs I had scored so far were in newspaper delivery and telemarketing. So, I took the university position. Little did I know at the time that it would shape my whole career.

How to Become a Consultant?

These examples illustrate the different ways of getting yourself in an IT consultant position. You must choose the right one for you. Remember that the application process does not start from submitting the job application. It starts much earlier when you plan on getting the right qualifications. And I do not merely mean earning a graduate degree with the most suitable major. Even if that ship has sailed, all hope is not lost. So keep on reading.

You should also know your preferences and personality to be able to choose the right companies and positions to apply to. You must do your homework researching the companies. Also, you should have the right expectations of how it will be to work as a newcomer in IT consulting. You cannot optimize everything, but you can achieve much by being organized in your job search.

In the best case, you will get into a position that will make a perfect starting point for your IT consulting career. And even if this is not the role of your dreams, you will be able to learn the ropes, clarify your preferences, and get the right credentials. That will allow you to take the next step towards your goal.

However, if you approach your job search in the wrong way, you can end up sending out tons of ill-targeted applications, losing valuable time for nothing. And even if you manage to score a job, it can be far from an ideal one for you. You will toil away in a boring or stressful position that does not take you one step closer to your dream job.

So, follow the advice in this chapter and get your dream job in IT consulting!

What Do the Companies Want From You?

You need to have the right qualifications to be considered for a position at an IT consultancy. Your employer must be able to sell you to client projects, so you must look credible enough. But what does this mean for you, and particularly your CV or resume? You should know the expectations before positioning yourself for your job search.

Recruiters have different expectations depending, for example, on the firm's size and the position of the person doing the recruiting. Of course, it also matters a great deal whether you are applying for your first job or have years of work experience. Let's look at some of the secrets of IT consulting recruiters!

Some Hire Consultants by the Dozen

Most large and some medium-sized companies are looking for "warm bodies." They just need someone who can handle the job and is, preferably, also a good fit in the organizational culture. You will be just one of the many hundreds or thousands of entries in the recruiting system. These companies do not expect you to be perfect and will not (and cannot) use much time to evaluate you. They do not stress too much if they can sell you to a client or not (they probably can, regardless of what you have in your CV or resume). They follow a standard recruiting process and guidelines for evaluating you. There are checklists to go through and standard questions to ask.

The preceding is even more so if the recruiter is someone from HR or some random person tasked for the job. If the person is not your future supervisor, they will not and probably even cannot evaluate you very thoroughly. If you pass certain criteria and there is a suitable position free, you are in. Even if there is no suitable position available, they might still take you if you are a good fit.

First, they will want to know if you will fit in the work culture. Second, they will try to evaluate if you have what it takes to work in the position you are applying to. Culturally, they will probably think you are a good fit if you appear pleasant enough, do not exhibit any of the attitudes listed earlier in the section "Is IT Consulting Really for You?", and can do some small talk. For suitability for the work part, they will check your degree, skills, and experience. What is important, then, depends on your seniority level.

In any case, having any skills that are currently in high demand is a major plus.

Some Will Do Hand-Picking

In smaller consultancies, the recruiter would probably be your manager (or work with you in some other way) if you are hired. Hiring a new employee is financially a big thing for a small company. They do not want to end up with an employee who is difficult to sell to clients, is work-shy, or just cannot handle the work. Therefore, they will investigate you more thoroughly. You will be evaluated as a person rather than just one of the many potential candidates.

They are looking for evidence that you are willing to work hard. This does not mean just appearing at work and staying there long enough. It means being able to create high-quality deliverables and to do it efficiently (remember that deliverables are central in this business). In tiny firms, you must also be able to work with little supervision, at least if you have some work experience. You must also convince the recruiter that you can take on new kinds of challenges.

Your CV or resume must look convincing to potential clients. These firms just cannot sneak you in as one of the many resources in a large project. And there are also interpersonal aspects to consider. Your recruiter must think he or she can work with you in case you are hired.

Entry-Level and Experienced Candidates

If you are applying for an entry-level position, the requirements are not high. Having a university degree takes you through the first check. Any relevant skills and work experience are a plus. Still, it is crucial to get the details right in your CV or resume. Every degree, training course, summer job, and skill counts. The point is to get your CV to look credible enough to get you to your first IT consulting job. From then on, it will get easier.

If you have already worked for ten years or more, the details get less important. Companies considering hiring you will look more at the big picture. Your degrees will count less and work experience more. You must have a solid work history with no unexplainable gaps. If you are already an IT professional, no one will pay much attention to the training you have taken or certificates you may have.

Being somewhere in the middle with, say, two years of work experience is closer to being an entry-level applicant. Your work experience is a definite plus if there is nothing suspicious about it. You should still try to polish your CV or resume, though.

What Are the Right Qualifications?

IT consulting firms are looking for candidates with certain qualifications. In this section, you will learn about the obvious and the not-so-obvious requirements.

It is easy to say that having a university degree and relevant work experience will help you tremendously in getting a job. You cannot change the facts without working for it for several years. But even if you currently do not have either, there are still actions you can take to optimize your qualifications—so read on!

However, if you are in the position of choosing what to study, there is more you can do to make yourself an excellent candidate for an IT consulting position. You will find useful information in the next section regarding your choice.

What Degree Should You Have?

If you want to play it safe, get a university or college degree (whether it should be bachelor's or master's depends on your country). Having one is almost a must for those looking for their first job, as recruiters highly respect these degrees. After all, what other criteria could you use for an entry-level candidate? Getting a degree shows, at least, that you can get things done. But it does not guarantee employment in any case.

I have spent my share of time in the university, earning my bachelor's, master's, and doctorate degrees. So, I can tell you this: most of the stuff you learn in a university is not applicable in consulting. Particularly, you spend much time studying the various theories related to your field of study. You will probably not need these in consulting. And most of the practical technical knowledge you may get in your studies probably gets obsolete before you graduate.

This is not to say that having a university degree is useless in your job. Actually, the most important thing that you learn in a university is an inquisitive and critical mindset. You will also learn some useful skills, such as those for information gathering, analysis, and presentation. Having such a degree can also be a plus when your company takes part in those public tenders that have the education of project members as a criterion—a university degree gets your CV or resume scored higher.

Your degree does not necessarily have to be about IT. My MSc is in economics. Does not sound very technical, right? At least I majored in information systems. My boss has an MSc in applied mathematics. Once, I even had a licensed physician as a colleague (he could give professional advice on the healthiest snacks for busy consultants. Apparently, a banana is the best choice). If you want a more relevant degree for the job, consider information systems, computer science, economics, organizational psychology, or anything about business.

Do not stress about your grades too much. My experience is that lower-than-perfect grades do not prevent you from getting a job (although some firms are known for hiring only the best of their class).

Earning a PhD is a double-edged sword (at many universities in Finland, you actually *get* a sword to go with the degree). Some clients, mostly in the public sector, may find such a degree a definite plus. However, if you spend several years in the university full-time to get one, some potential employers may consider you too theoretical—if they do not have a reason to believe otherwise. Getting work experience from somewhere other than a university alleviates this effect.

Of course, if you do not have a university degree, it will take several years to earn one. If this is the case for you, the question is whether you should get a degree before applying to your first IT consulting position. I would advise you not to do that, at least if you do not want the degree for some other reason. Instead, get other qualifications and then apply for that job. After all, you may decide that you do not like the field at all—after having spent years (and probably also money) to get your degree.

What About Your Work Experience?

If you are already working and are considering a career change, you might think about whether your work experience is relevant for the new job. Almost any kind of IT work experience is relevant if you choose the right position to apply to. There are also many people working in the industry who have no IT background before moving into IT consulting.

For example, experience in business, management, politics, or a particular industry can be very valuable for IT consultants. It also depends on what kind of IT consultant you want to be. For example, if you want to focus on a certain industry, knowing it inside out may be much more valuable than any technical know-how. And even if your focus is rather technical, it is still not a drawback to know your business. Also, the networks you bring with you to your new work can be extremely valuable.

If you are just finishing your studies, *any* kind of work experience is a plus. So be sure to mention all those summer jobs, even if they have nothing to do with the industry. Work is work, anyway. Working in a position of responsibility (for example, the chairman or the treasurer) in an association or club is also valuable experience. If you have hobbies relevant for your future job (such as coding), be sure to mention those as well (preferably with examples and even work samples). It is a definite plus if you can show that you are interested in working on such things even in your spare time.

For several years during my studies, during summer and Christmas holidays, I woke up in the small hours to deliver newspapers for the Finnish Post, six days a week. This kind of work really makes you appreciate a desk job, but at least I was pretty fit after running all those stairs up and down. Later, I sold mobile and broadband subscriptions by phone. I had these jobs in my CV until I got my first IT consultant job.

Last, a word of warning. Public sector organizations and universities may have a rather different work culture than companies. If this is true in your country and you have been working in one of these organizations, be prepared for a culture change. If you have been working in such an organization for too long, the change may even be too much for you. Consequently, some recruiters may even think you are already too "tainted" for the consulting business—but it is not that simple. If you apply to a consultancy with many public sector clients, work experience from the public sector can be valuable. Such clients will probably appreciate that you do not merely have work experience from consulting.

What Skills Do You Need?

In addition to the right work experience, certain skills are valued in IT consulting. Work in IT consulting is project work. Working in a project as a team is probably the most important experience you can have. But note that pure project managers grow on trees in the consulting business (although *good* project managers do not). It is better to have some other specialty as well or be exceedingly good at what you do.

Who in today's workplaces has not worked in at least a few projects? If you are still studying, try to get into a student project or two. There may even be courses where you do real project work (such as IT solutions development) for real clients. So, highlight your project experience, preferably with examples.

Common IT skills go without saying. Yes, you must be fluent with office tools and know your way around a laptop. There are, of course, many different technical skills that may be required in IT consulting. Depending on your specialty, you should know the tools and work practices of your trade (remember to mention their names in your CV or resume). If you are applying to a junior position, you are not expected to have much practical knowledge on the subject matter.

As brought out, communication and influencing skills, at large, are important in consulting. They are the basic skills for almost any consultant. If you have nurtured your skills in, say, information-gathering, writing, presenting, networking, or lobbying—they are probably all relevant. There are, of course, many ways to learn these skills. Some of them include, for example, leading people, teaching, doing scientific research, and politics. So, take all opportunities you can to improve these skills!

When it comes to more technical skills, you can focus on the currently sought-after skills—if you want to do some optimizing. Of course, it is even better to start learning skills that will be valuable in the near future—but knowing such things in advance is a rather unusual talent. Even a little experience helps. When clients start requesting such experts by the boatload, IT consultancies must start hiring people off the street. If you can profile yourself well, you will get the job.

At the time of writing, these hot skills include, for example, anything related to artificial intelligence (AI) or data analytics. Also, cybersecurity skills continue to be in demand. So, look around for opportunities in contributing to a project dealing with such a hot topic. Maybe the company you work for is initiating an AI pilot project? Or your university has a course where you can do some hands-on work on analytics? Also, consider doing your thesis on such a topic, preferably in cooperation with some company.

Working or getting a university degree (or any degree, for that matter) is not the only way to get the necessary know-how. There are so many free educational resources on the internet that you can study practically anything without getting a formal degree. You may even get a certificate to show to your future employer.

It is all well and good to list your skills in your CV. Still, you should consider how to make it look credible. They should reflect your responsibilities and accomplishments at work or be related to your studies. Skills learned by self-study are more difficult to justify. Pointing the recruiter to some public examples of your work may help.

Get Certified

Consider getting a relevant certificate or two. A certificate is a concrete credential to put in your CV or resume. There are numerous certifications in the field of IT. Having one basically shows that you know the essentials of a particular methodology or technology. Certificates are generally easy to get, but some consultancies and clients think highly of them. Having a relevant certificate is important, especially if you are at the beginning of your career or want to specialize. Certification authorities advertise how much you will earn if you get their certificate, but it is not that simple.

Usually, you take an exam to get certified. There may also be other requirements. You can study for the certification exam yourself or take a dedicated course. Taking the certification exam costs 300 € or more (more than a thousand if you attend the course).

To get started, google for certifications in your field. If you do not have a specialty, get one of the more generic certificates. For example, IT service management, data management, agile solutions development, and information security are useful topics for any IT professional. If there are many relevant options, you should compare their focus, price, and requirements and select the most appropriate for you.

Know Your Preferences

Before applying for any job, you should spend some time thinking about your preferences. That way, you can make a more informed choice on which companies to apply to. You will get a head start in your career if you choose the company and position that best suits your goals, personality, working style, and other preferences. Avoiding the most obvious mistakes also saves you from stress.

That is the theory, anyway. I know it is difficult to say what kind of IT consulting work or company you would like if you have not even worked in the industry. You just do not know for certain if you will like something if you have not tried it. During my studies, I did not even consider myself to be the "consultant type." And look where I ended up. One of the points of this book is to help you choose by telling you what is available and possible.

Even if you are applying for your first job, you can still set goals for your career. But when it comes to preferences, there are two aspects that you should put weight on. First, the job must look good in your CV or resume. Second, you must be able to grow as an IT consultant in the job. For example, does your role allow you to learn new things? Would you get a coach who can help you to improve your skills? So, keep these in mind during your job search.

If you already have work experience, the situation is different. In that case, you should have an idea of what you can and like to do at work. Therefore, you can have some preferences for your first job in IT consulting.

To help you define your preferences, I have brought out some topics which I think are the most significant. The first two sections are relevant for both entry-level and experienced job seekers. After that, there is a section for those with more work experience.

So, go through the following sections and write down some bullet points for each. If nothing comes up, do not worry. Just jump to the next section.

What Do You Want From Work?

People usually recommend spending some time thinking about your goals before beginning any major endeavor. This also applies to your career. Having goals will help you focus your efforts better and find the right direction whenever there is a choice to be made. It is also the starting point for understanding your preferences for your work and workplace.

So, think about what you would like to achieve in your IT consulting career. It may help to think broadly. What do you want in life? Work is one of the tools to achieve that. There are plenty of online resources to help you with this. Just google for "what is your why."

You can have both short-term and long-term goals. At this point, they do not even have to be specific, measurable, or even realistic.

Just write down whatever comes to mind. Here are some examples:

- I want to be the CEO in 10–20 years.
- I want to be the number one expert in the firm in my specialty.
- I want to be an internal consultant who advises many projects.
- I want to find new clients and open new areas of business.
- I want to travel a lot on business.
- I do not want to travel on business.
- I want to get enough consulting experience to start my own company.
- I want to earn a lot, so I can retire at 40.
- I want to get to know many people.
- I want to work nine to five.
- I want to earn just enough to cover my expenses and work as little as possible.

A final point about goals: it helps if you can pin down why you want to achieve your goals as an IT consultant specifically. You need this to justify your motivation for applying for such a position. It also pays to revisit your career choice once more after you have thought about your goals.

How Much Do You Want to Work?

When it comes to working hours, there is quite a diversity in the industry. There are those consultancies where it is possible and even culturally okay to work nine to five. There are even workplaces which allow you to work shorter than normal hours, say, only four days a week (naturally, this is reflected in the salary).

Then, there are the consultancies where you must work your ass off. Like the work culture in management consulting, some firms expect you to put in 50 or even 80 hours a week. Then there is overtime to consider. Even if you theoretically have normal work hours, you may be expected to do overtime regularly.

So, think about your situation and priorities for a minute. Will you give everything to your work (at least for some time), or do you want a more balanced work-life?

What Do You Want to Do?

If you already have work experience, you can think about your preferences for your IT consulting job a bit further.

You can start by thinking about your current and former jobs for a minute. What are you good at? What kind of work do you enjoy? How do you like to work? The purpose of this exercise is to pin down the kind of roles you would like to work in IT consulting (check the information in the chapter "Know the Consulting Business" for reference). This will help you to select the most suitable position and company for you.

You can also use the following dimensions to narrow down your preferences. When it comes down to evaluating IT consulting positions and employers, I have found them the most significant. Naturally, these things are not black and white, but you can probably choose the side that describes you best.

- **Are you a manager or an expert?** Managers focus on managing teams, projects, organizational units, and companies. Subject-matter experts, then, are the individuals who do the actual work. Having a preference on this is perhaps the most important consideration for your IT consulting career. Managers should aim for medium-sized and large consultancies. Experts may fit in anywhere, but there are also great differences between companies.
- **Are you a generalist or a specialist?** Generalists can handle many of the different tasks involved in a typical IT solution implementation project, or in other kinds of projects. On the other hand, specialists focus on a particular type of work, technology, or client industry. Generalists have better opportu-

nities in larger consultancies, while specialists thrive in a boutique consultancy or a medium-sized firm with the right specialization.

- **What is your specialization?** Specializations can be wide or narrow (or anything in between). Some have a quite large specialization (for example, I work on different types of architecture in many different contexts), but a specialization nonetheless (I would not like to be staffed as a coder or a project manager, for example). Then there are the ones with a very narrow specialization, such as configuring a specific brand of packaged software. You can, of course, have several specializations.

- **Do you want to work in large or small projects?** Large IT solution implementations can involve several projects, with dozens of individuals staffed in each. On the other hand, other types of IT consulting projects are significantly smaller. For example, a project for advisory work can be staffed by only one or two people. Large companies tend to have large projects.

- **Do you want to take part in your company's internal work?** Are you interested in doing sales support, content marketing, or other types of internal work for your company? If this is an important consideration for you, there is a better chance for this kind of work in small consultancies.

When you are at it, you should also think about the future. Are you certain that your preferences will be the same in, say, five years? If you are willing to try something new, that is also a preference you should consider. Naturally, the Consulting Titans have the best variety of work opportunities.

Update Your CV or Resume and LinkedIn Profile

When you have set your preferences, it is time to update your CV (in the US, it is called a resume). Even in the 2020s, with video applications and job searches by social media, a traditional CV is still the thing recruiters look for. You should always have an up-to-date CV, which you can then tailor for different applications. And when you have a great CV, you can use its content also in your LinkedIn profile.

There are plenty of resources available to help you with your CV. For example, Indeed and ResumeGenius have useful step-by-step guides with examples. The latter even has a resume builder app. So, I will here focus on my experience on CVs and point you to useful resources. If you are not sure if you can still create a credible CV, it may pay to get coaching. You can also ask for feedback from friends and colleagues and even from your LinkedIn network.

The mass of well-meaning advice can mislead you. Some of it is plain wrong or not appropriate to your country. There is only so much you can do to polish your CV to make up for, for example, short work history or one with unexplainable gaps. If you use every trick in the book to make your CV look good, there is a risk that you will sound desperate. It is the same as having a tattoo on your forehead saying, "looking for a job."

So, if you are just about to graduate and look for a job, let your CV show the situation. Be sure to tell about your achievements but be humble. You probably cannot be an expert in anything—yet. Of course, there are cultural differences, but at least where I come from, no-one will take you seriously if you think too highly of yourself. Experienced recruiters will see through your CV. Relax. It is totally fine to be looking for your first job. If you sell yourself to your future employer as a superman or a superwoman, you will get caught if you do not live up to the promises. There is a thing called a probation period. At least smaller companies will readily use their option to terminate your employment if you cannot deliver what you lead them to expect.

The same goes for experienced jobseekers. You should bring things out in good light. You can even leave things out. But do not exaggerate. Being in terms with your company's CIO or even CEO does not make you a "trusted advisor of the C-suite." Do not fill your CV with claims that have no basis in your work history. If you have gaps in your work history, do not make up "assignments" to fill them. You will not get far by lying.

Rather, let your accomplishments speak for themselves. If you can say, for example, that you managed an enterprise-wide enterprise resource planning system implementation from initiation to deployment, you do not have to say much else. You will get instant credibility. The achievements can even be something you consider very small. Any achievement related to leadership, organizing, project work, or international aspects is probably relevant.

You can do a lot by just structuring your CV clearly and making it look neat. Get someone with an eye for design to do it for you if you are unsure or use a good-quality template. Some advise *not* to include a photo in your CV, but I would do it anyway if it is not explicitly forbidden. You should have the photo taken professionally. And remember, when it comes to the length of your CV, less is more.

All the stuff here also applies to your LinkedIn profile. There are plenty of resources to help you but be critical. For example, The Balance Careers has an informative article with further links, and The Muse has a list of useful tips. It is even easier to overdo it with your LinkedIn profile than with your CV. So take it easy with those emoticons! Many recommend using a personal and informal style. That probably helps, but I have also had success with a somewhat dry profile summary. It might also be a good idea to make a one-page CV summary to be shared on LinkedIn with potential employers.

Choose Your Strategy

If you got this far, you have already set some preferences for your future IT consulting position. Next, it is time to consider how to get it. Sending out masses of job applications is hardly the only way to get a job in the industry. Many people use their network to their advantage. Sometimes, the companies even come to you. Use the information in the following sections to plan your approach.

The Old-Fashioned Way

Applying the traditional way involves the choice between an open application and applying for a position. Applying for a position is a good option if a suitable position is available and you can profile yourself well for it.

Open applications tend to be more of a lottery. Success depends, for example, on whether or not the company is currently recruiting a lot of new people. If you have a great CV or get lucky, it might work.

Get a Referral

The easiest way to get a job is by utilizing your network. One way to take advantage of it is to find a person to refer you to the company you are interested in. For example, if you have a friend or a colleague who works in such a company, you can ask for a referral and multiply your chances of getting picked. That is why it is a good idea to keep up with your colleagues and people you studied with. During my years in IT consulting, I have referred a couple of friends (one even got the job). Some companies may offer a reward for the referee if the candidate gets picked. So there is even an extra incentive to refer you. Of course, your referee must think you are a good enough candidate.

You can also ask for a referral indirectly. Perhaps your fellow student or colleague knows someone in an interesting company. He or she could get you to an interview directly, past the queue. You can even ask for a referral on LinkedIn. In any case, the person you are asking for a referral should know you and have a good impression of you. No one will refer some random person.

This approach obviously limits your choices. You really must have an extensive network in the industry to know a potential referee in every interesting consulting firm. You probably must weigh convenience over the range of options. Also, you should consider if the company really is suitable for your preferences. The fact that you can get a referral does not necessarily mean that you should use that option.

Lure the Recruiters to You Online

Having an excellent LinkedIn profile and being active on LinkedIn is something you should be doing anyway (Twitter is another social media channel professionals use). Headhunters, recruiting consultants, and companies' own recruiters are always looking for suitable candidates on LinkedIn. Everyone recommends building your personal brand online, but it is, of course, more easily said than done. In practice, regularly posting relevant content and commenting on others' posts increases your chances of getting noticed. But remember that whatever you do on LinkedIn should bring you out in good light as a professional. For example, complaining about the bad service you got from some firm may get your post likes and visibility but does not necessarily build your professional brand. Also, remember to tag relevant skills (they are essential) and set your profile open for a job.

Several years ago, a headhunter was contacting me every month or so through LinkedIn. I had a decent, but not perfect, profile. At the time, I also seldom posted anything. So, in addition to having an okay profile, there is not much you have to do to get contacted. Nowadays, there is still the occasional message, even though having partner in my title seems to drive recruiters away efficiently.

You do not have to wait passively for someone to find you. You can contact headhunters and recruiting consultants yourself. And why not connect directly with people from the companies you are interested in? Remember to add a personal message to the invite and follow the LinkedIn etiquette also in other respects.

If you are unemployed or looking for your first job, why not just ask for one on LinkedIn? I have seen this approach work several times in my network. See the tips on writing applications later in this chapter to get your post to stand out. You should also ask friends and acquaintances to like, comment, and share your post. This increases its visibility tremendously.

The Power of Good Impression

As said before, this is how I got my job at Coala. If you work closely with someone and leave a good impression, he or she may well remember you after parting ways. And when your colleague needs to recruit someone, you may be high on the list. This may happen even years later — for me, it was about two years after.

The same may also happen in a client-consultant relationship. It is no secret that both consultants and client representatives may be looking for potential recruits. Usually, consultants are lured by their clients, but I have also seen consultancies hire client people several times.

There are usually clauses against such behavior in the contract, so neither party can openly recruit the other's employees. But anything your company signs probably does not prevent you, as an employee, from seeking new employment. So, if you work with consultants as a client representative, also keep this possibility in mind. No consultant will probably ask you directly, but he or she may give subtle hints. It is up to you to ask if there would be a place for you in the consultancy.

How Many Companies to Apply To?

You also must choose if you will be applying to one or several companies at a time. If you get several job offers, you can run the potential employers against each other to get a better deal. That is the theory, anyway. To get into such a position, you need to have skills that are in high demand or an otherwise strong CV. Different companies also take different lengths of time to process your application, so you might not even be able to get the job offers simultaneously. Some companies take weeks, some even months, to arrive at a decision. Remember, you can end up with *no* job if you try to squeeze too much or take too long to optimize your choices. In any case, it will be wearing to handle several interviews (sometimes on the same day). You will also need to be organized about it to be able to remember what you have discussed at each of the firms and at which point of the application process you are in each of them.

You can also do as I did. Apply to one company only and see how it goes before applying to anywhere else. This approach has its good sides. It makes you appear serious about applying for that job (make sure this comes out in the interview). It also saves your time, as you send out only one application at a time.

I do not recommend sending out dozens of applications at once. It takes time and effort to research the companies and create good applications. You will probably start cutting corners. Copy-pasting leads to generic applications. In the end, you will lose time for nothing.

If you do not have much experience on job applications and interviews or are just unsure of how you will perform in an interview, there is an approach you can try. A colleague suggested making a "dry-run" application for some not-so-interesting position, just for practice's sake, before applying for the position you are actually interested in. You get to practice creating a perfect application and CV, and hopefully, also try out a job interview—and learn from it.

What Did I Love About My Job at the Consulting Titan?

Now, I will offer you a shortcut for your job search. Take it, and you can avoid much of the work involved in finding the best companies to apply to. If you decide to do this, just read the following and skip the next section in this chapter.

Interested in getting off light? That's what I thought. Just do like I did and choose the one Consulting Titan that sounds the best for you—and apply there (preferably to that one company only). You will have all the chances of getting a great start in your consulting career. Even if you do not like it, you will gain valuable experience and get many of the benefits of working for one of the world's most prestigious consultancies. Then, use your new-gained experience to make a more informed choice when applying for the next job.

As said, you cannot go much wrong by going for one of the Consulting Titans. If you apply for your first job, one of these companies will make an excellent starting point for your career. Even many career changers may find working for one of these firms an excellent choice.

Here are my reasons for going for one of the large, well-known consultancies.

- **Excellent onboarding**. These companies make sure that you know the basics before you are put in a client project. There are well-designed programs to get new joiners up to speed. They will teach you what you need to know about the company's procedures and policies. You will also get training in consulting skills and even in the subject matter. There are coaches to support you.

- **Variety of work**. Working for one of these companies is the best way to get an overview of the different types of projects and clients in the industry. You get to try out different kinds of work. This is extremely valuable for those new in consulting, as it is the only way for you to know what you will like.

- **Inspiring people**. The individuals you will work with in these companies are motivated, hardworking, smart, and easy to get along with. Your managers generally know what they are doing. There are, of course, exceptions, but they are not many.

- **Learning opportunities**. The variety of roles and increasing challenges make sure that you *must* learn a lot. Also, there are loads of training courses you can take. Constant support and a beginner-friendly environment make it relatively safe to try out new things. You get experience and knowledge that are worth a lot wherever your career takes you.

- **Free-time activities**. I have already mentioned the parties, outings, and other communal events. There are also clubs for different interests. I was a long-time member of the Boardgame Club. We had a respectable collection of games (all paid by the company) and just the right amount of people. I even kept coming to the gaming events for years after leaving the company! I was also the founding member of the Aero Club. In addition to the obvious sightseeing flights with single-engine planes, we went ballooning. We also got to fly three flight simulators they use to train pilots at the Finnair Flight Academy. There were also clubs for various sports, wine, and even cigars.

- **Fair terms of employment**. There is no question about it that these firms want you to give them your best. Still, this does not have to mean working longer than normal days—at least without being paid extra for it. When you consider the terms in your contract, they are pretty much what you would get somewhere else. There may be some atypical clauses, but I have seen worse. If you consider the benefits, the deal seems fair.

- **Looks great in your CV or resume**. These companies are well-known and respected. They do not hire just anyone, and just anyone cannot succeed in them. By having worked for one of these companies, *your* credibility will get a boost. Even if you eventually want to work in some obscure boutique consultancy, it pays to get an entry from a well-known consultancy first.

Create Your Shortlist

You should not just be throwing out job applications to every IT consulting company you can imagine. This way, the applications tend to be rather generic and not very well customized for each company and position. Also, it is much trouble to copy-paste your personal information to masses of applications. And you would not like to work just any-where anyway.

You should be focused in your job search. Here, I will tell you how to create a shortlist of companies to apply to.

Make a Preliminary List

First, you should understand roughly the type of company that is the best fit for you. Use your goals and preferences, and information in chapter "Know the Companies" as a guide. Then, select the type of company you would like to apply to.

The plan is to make a preliminary list of companies and positions you are interested in. Besides the company's type, you should also limit your search geographically to wher-ever you want to work (sometimes, there can be limited options available if you are not willing to move or can work remotely). If you first do this kind of rough filtering, you will save time in the next step, where you will find out more about the companies. At this point, you should prob-ably have no more than ten companies on your list.

Just start searching for suitable companies and posi-tions. It is easy to find the Consulting Titans and the most well-known medium-sized consultancies in your country. But the smaller the company, the harder it is to find (and even harder to research in the next step). Here are some ideas where to look for potential employers:

- **Google it**. The internet is obviously a good starting point. For example, if you are interested in applying to one of the Consulting Titans in your country, google for "top consulting companies <add country name here>" (or your local language equivalent). A more targeted search is in order to find boutique consultancies (for example, "enterprise architecture consulting helsinki").

- **Company review and survey websites**. There are international and local websites with rankings of the best employers in the field, based on employee reviews. Then there are employer surveys, such as the Great Place to Work, that also indicate which companies may be worth looking into.

- **Job search websites**. If you want to look for suitable positions first and companies second, job search websites such as Glassdoor and Indeed are an excellent starting point. Also, check any local job search websites in your country.

- **LinkedIn**. According to some of my colleagues, LinkedIn is the best channel for searching for an IT job. You can set search filters according to your preferences. When you find an interesting company, begin to follow it. You should also follow content related to your work interests in your news stream. You can also directly ask your network for ideas on potential employers. Of course, it takes time to build a sufficient network. But it can be extremely valuable for finding boutique consultancies that fly below the radar in other media.

- **Local business and IT magazines**. I do not mean meticulously going through the archives. Just pay attention to any content on IT consulting companies in the magazines you read anyway. If none are on your reading list, you should start following a few local, high-quality ones. Look for listings and articles about IT consulting companies. For example, a particular magazine for IT professionals regularly publishes a listing of the 250 largest IT companies in Finland.

- **Career fairs and other recruiting events**. Large and well-known consultancies hold a steady presence in the most important recruiting events. They are also active in recruiting students directly from the university. These events are extremely valuable, as you can get first-hand information on how it is to work for the company. You may also get a referral. I learned about my first IT consulting employer by attending an event with a sauna (obviously), drinks, and snacks, organized by university alumni now working in the company. Later, I kept up the tradition by helping to organize a few such events myself.

- **Friends and acquaintances**. Put your network to use! You can get valuable information from people working in the consulting business or even in an organization that hires consultants. For example, contact colleagues and people you studied with. It never hurts to ask. And while you are at it, consider who in your network could be your employment references for each job you are interested in.

Do Your Research

After you have the preliminary list, do a little more research on each of the companies. This will help you to find out if the company is the right one for you. And you should anyway know the basics about the companies to target your application and be able to ask the right questions in the interview.

I did very little research beforehand for my first IT consulting workplace. So there were some surprises. I recommend not making the same mistake. The time spent on research is well spent. It also saves you time and effort because you can leave out companies you do not want to apply anyway.

Research involves checking the basics, such as what the company does and how well it does financially. You should also be on the lookout for any information that could tell whether the company meets your goals and preferences. You can use this to evaluate the company against your preferences.

Be as organized in this step as you want. For example, you can jot down pluses and minuses for each potential employer. You can even rate the companies against each of your preferences (for example, on a scale of one to five). Just do not put too much effort into this. Remember that even if you do your homework well, it only goes so far. In the end, you will only find out the truth about the company after you have worked there for a while.

There is still one thing you can do while researching your options. When you find an interesting company, write down any questions you would like to know the answers for. You cannot find all the answers yourself, anyway. You can then ask these questions when you get to the interview part.

Here are some of the properties you should investigate:

- **Business**. You should know what the company does, in which geographies it operates, what kind of clients it has, and how large it is. See what information you can find about the company's services and products and what it specializes in. It may be difficult to get to the specifics through the jargon, though. There are many kinds of IT consulting, so make sure that the business looks interesting and fits your preferences. Also, the location of the closest office may be a deciding factor for you.

- **Finances**. You will also want to know how the company is doing financially, especially if it is an obscure non-listed firm. Avoid joining one that is on the verge of bankruptcy. There are many facets to a company's finances, but at least check the turnover (sales) and net income. The first indicates the size of the business, and the second if it turns a profit (it should be a positive number). You can also compare these numbers between companies.

- **Compensation and benefits**. Find out about the salary level for the position you are planning to apply for. Also, check what benefits are available.
- **Work time expectations**. If this is an important point for you, try to find out how much people are expected to work in the company.
- **Open positions**. Check what positions are currently open in the company. Write down any that interest you and fit your preferences. Applying to a trainee or intern position is a good option for those fresh out of university. Many large consultancies have programs for taking in new graduates (and even ones who have not yet graduated) with various terms of employment. These jobs can last a few months or more and may lead to permanent employment. The requirements for candidates are not overwhelming, but there is much competition. So, the more important it is to get your CV and application right.
- **Reputation.** You want to know if the company you are considering is a good employer and carries itself in an ethical way. You can use many sources of information, including (but not limited to) friends and acquaintances, company review websites, and news articles. There may be some strong opinions out there but remember to form your own opinion based on multiple information sources.

- **Culture and values**. Working in the wrong kind of culture can get strenuous. So, in a perfect world, you should evaluate the company against your cultural preferences and values. In practice, this is impossible to do before you have worked in the company for several years. But you can still do your best. Knowing your preferences, ask people in your network a couple of questions on the most important points. Also, check the company's values to find out if there is something you do not like.

Where should you then search for this information? The company's website is a good starting point. It probably has useful information, for example, on the company's finances, products and services, locations, clients, and values. Take a critical stance against any stories about working in the company if it is part of the company's official communication. That is usually just marketing material that does not give you a realistic picture of how it is there.

Company review and compensation research websites can be handy. Glassdoor, Indeed, and PayScale are some examples of these. However, the international ones may not have information relevant to your country. So be sure also to check if there are any local ones in your country. Reviews in Google Maps can also give you some clues, but look at the big picture, not individual reviews. For news articles, use Google or check the largest newspaper in your country.

Also, ask for experiences from those friends and acquaintances who have worked in the company or a similar one. For example, someone in your university alumni network may be able to help you. You can also use the search feature on LinkedIn to find people who have the company in their CVs. However, discussing salary may be taboo in some cultures, so watch out. If you have specific questions, you can also ask the contact person mentioned in the job posting.

For financial data, go no further than annual reports. Besides numbers, they also have information in text on what the company does, how the business is going, and what its prospects are. Be sure to check these from the last three or so years. For listed companies, you can probably get the reports for free from the internet. Some websites provide you with just the essential numbers. For example, check Yahoo Finance. For annual reports of non-listed companies, see the organization that registers companies in your country.

Make the Choice

When you think that you know enough about the companies on your shortlist, stop. During the research, you might have even identified a few new companies to add to your list. Depending on your strategy, select one or more companies to apply to. You can also put the companies in order of preference. As a final check, for each company, make the critical question: would you really want to work there? If not, drop the company from the list.

Create an Excellent Application

When you have your list of companies ready, it is time to apply. Unless your potential employer wants to drag you from your home to the job interview, you will need to apply for the job. Again, there is plenty of material on the internet about writing applications and cover letters. The article at Indeed is a useful example. You cannot go much wrong by heeding the advice that comes up in multiple sources.

Here are some points I would like to make based on my experience and knowledge of job applications.

Select the Position

The first thing to remember is to apply only to positions (and companies) that interest you (a dry-run application for the sake of practicing is an exception). If you have found several good options, apply to those that seem to be the best fit for your preferences. Depending on your strategy, you may send out one or many applications. If you want to start it easy, begin with one well-targeted application.

Target Your Application

Targeting means forming your message specifically for the position and company in mind. Applications that look copy-pasted will be passed quickly. This means tailoring both your application and CV (or resume) specifically for each case. The bulk of your CV can be reused if you have targeted it for IT consulting to begin with, but you should write your CV summary for each application.

If you apply for an open position, it is easier to target your application. If there is no suitable position to apply, but the company is a good fit for you, try sending an open application. In that case, target your application to the company and what it does.

One way to target your application is to use the requirements for the position as a checklist. Construct your CV and application in a way that they communicate that you meet the key requirements. Just do not be too obvious about it. You can highlight a few of the key traits in the application and in the summary of your CV, but do not answer the requirements one by one. Just make sure that the information is there. Also, companies put all kinds of ridiculous requirements in their position descriptions, so you do not have to answer nearly all of them.

Profile Yourself

Your application and CV should tell a convincing story about yourself and your career. Your profile describes your experience, skills, and specialties and how you conduct yourself in your business. It can be thought of as your personal brand. The point of profiling is to get your future employer to see that you are the right person specifically for the job you are applying to. You must communicate that you are not just any random, generic IT (or business) person but a professional with specific strengths. It is better to have focus than to be a generalist who will do anything. This way, your profile does not, of course, fit all positions and companies, but you will have a better chance in the ones where it does.

So, tell specifically what you can and want to do. This may be difficult if you are just about to finish your studies, but at least you can tell what interests you and how your skills and experience support it. Especially, you should tell why you want to be a consultant. There are plenty of reasons mentioned earlier in this book that you can use. Mix in some of your passions and career goals, and your profile is all set.

If you have work experience, you should also include a career story. It is a short narrative that points out what kind of work you have done and why. Basically, take each employment from your work history and tell a bit about the subject matter of your work, what you have learned, and why you have changed jobs (if you have).

Stand Out From the Masses

In addition to profiling yourself well, you can also take other actions to make your application stand out. You can try the following to do that.

- **Tell something personal about yourself**. This provides something to remember you by. So add one or two funny and/or convincing personal details about yourself. Talking about your hobby or passion in an interesting way is a typical example. People are fascinated with traveling and other international experiences, so these are always good topics to boast about. Mentioning a highlight, such as appearing on a TV show or winning (or losing) in an important sports competition, can also bring you out in good light. These may even offer a topic to have small talk about in the interview.

- **Add a link to your blog**. A work-related blog or a set of professional articles can showcase your professional point-of-views and writing skills nicely.

- **Add a link to social media**. Probably Facebook is out of the question. But guiding the recruiters to your LinkedIn and Twitter profiles may be a plus if you have posted relevant content.

- **Make a video**. Sometimes employers specifically ask for a video application. Still, you can make one in any case (be sure also to include a written one if they ask for that). A video gives an example of your presentation skills. Going through the trouble also shows that you are serious about your application.

- **Share a work sample**. Why not share some concrete examples of your work? Depending on the position you are applying to, these can be, for example, websites, applications, or designs. I have seen a job applicant bring an iPad loaded with architecture diagrams to a job interview. I, and others, were impressed. Ensure that your samples can be shared publicly, and do not cheat by sharing someone else's work.

Give Justified Salary Requirements

Companies may ask for your salary requirements. These should be higher than you would earn but not outrageously high. My salary requirement for my first IT consulting job was about 1 000 euros higher (per month, before tax) than I would initially get. Obviously, this did not hinder me from getting the job.

It is risky to suggest anything if you do not have a clue what individuals usually earn in such a position. Use the websites mentioned earlier to find out about the salary level. For more generic salary information, you can find articles dealing with IT consultant salaries.

If asked for a justification why you should be earning that much, referring to the general salary level is not the right answer. So, think of a justification related to *you* just in case. It is probably difficult to think of one if you are fresh from school. Your skills and experience are a good starting point.

Ace the Job Interview

When you get invited to one, it is time to start preparing for it. Preparing for and attending interviews can be strenuous. That is one more reason to apply only to the minimum number of positions. Those willing to run potential employers against each other have the arduous task of going through several interviews (if they get to that phase, that is).

In some companies, you also have to take an aptitude test. Personally, I have never had to take one when applying for a job. If I applied for a new job, I would avoid employers that require one (interviewing me and checking my CV should be more than enough). Still, those applying for their first job cannot be so picky. In many companies, the policy states that all recruitment candidates have to take an aptitude test (for whatever reason; it certainly does not prevent recruiting unsuitable employees). So, you have to decide for yourself if you want to put an effort on going through a test. Also, remember that companies also take longer to process your application when a test is involved. And if you do not get a favorable test result, it is not the end of your career. Just apply somewhere else.

The many resources available on succeeding in an interview (and in an aptitude test) have relevant information you should put into practice. Indeed provides some useful tips for a job interview, but there are many other resources as well. Next, let's have a look at the things I have found relevant.

Know the Basics

Knowing the basics about the company should already be more than covered if you have followed the advice earlier in this chapter. When it comes to the subject matter related to the position you are applying to, do not expect to be tested too much on that in the interview.

If you have work experience, expect the conversation on the subject matter to focus on what you have done and what you have learned. If you are fresh from the university, your interviewees do not even expect you to know much on the subject matter. Still, it helps to know the key concepts relevant to the position.

Look and Act Like a Consultant

There are certain expectations towards how IT consultants should look. So, appear to the interview dressed like one. Only a few world-renowned IT consulting rock stars can appear at the client's wearing a hoodie and Crocks. When job interviews are considered, underdressing is much worse than overdressing.

There are, of course, differences between countries, companies, and clients on how you are expected to look. I wear a button-up shirt, jeans, and semi-smart shoes almost anywhere I go (I sometimes add a jacket for an improved first impression). For men, a conservatively colored suit without a tie (the official technology consultant uniform as I know it) is probably a safe choice for an interview. Women should look for something in the lines of business casual. And sorry if this is obvious for you, but please, take care of your personal hygiene (men, this also includes getting a haircut and a beard trim).

When it comes to acting like a consultant, begin with appearing at the interview well in time. Arriving ten minutes early is fine; make it twenty if you want to play it safe. You cannot do much worse than be late. Conduct yourself in a friendly and courteous manner (remember, this is a service business). You do not have to act overly formal, but do not be too informal, either.

With all the advice here and elsewhere, there is only so much you can actually take into practice. You should also look natural. For example, you should not just keep saying things you have memorized or have an act on. Be yourself. Even IT consultancies are looking for people and not human robots.

Do Not Mess Up Your Profile

Everything you say in the interview should support the story you have started with your application and CV. You should have a career goal that you can communicate. Every employer also wants to know that you want to progress in your career, are willing to learn, and are a team player.

Do not be absolute in your opinions. For example, it is not a good idea to say that you would never like to be a manager. Better leave all options open. You can also check the company's values for hints about what characteristics they are looking for and then communicate a matching story. However, that should not be inconsistent with how you are—it will show. And do not overdo it.

Ask the Right Questions

Questions have two purposes in a job interview. Asking the right questions makes you seem smart and interested. There may also be things you genuinely want to know about your potential future job. So feel free to ask a lot of questions.

I would advise you to skip questions that have obvious answers. For example, it serves no purpose to ask about something you can read from the company's web page. Rather, ask about matters that are important or are even game changers for you. Your research on the company probably left you with blanks you would like to fill. Focus on topics that have to do with your preferences. It is better to avoid asking too difficult questions or ones that the interviewer may interpret as critical. For example, if the company has recently been in the news in a negative way, you probably gain nothing by touching that topic (they have heard enough about it). And do not get too personal with the interviewer (but you can still ask for experiences and opinions on work-related matters).

With all the stress of the interview, you may forget about an important topic to dive into. It is not forbidden to bring notes with you. Having a list of intelligent questions written down may even make you seem more professional. Even consultants cannot keep everything in their heads. As a consultant, you must be an effective note-taker and organized with your notes.

Here are some topics you might want to ask about in a job interview:

- **Compensation**. You will probably want to know how much you would be earning. So why not ask it directly if the topic does not otherwise come up? Your compensation usually consists of a base salary and a bonus. The bonus incentive is more aggressive in some cases. The bonus can be based on your personal performance or some company-level criteria. Your billing (the monetary value of your work billed from clients) is an often-used criterion. Many kinds of pay models are used in consultancies, so you should understand how your total compensation is determined and how you can affect it. Higher base salary and lower bonus mean that you know beforehand how much you will be earning each month. There might also be a sign-up bonus, but do not let it draw your attention away from the salary.

- **Benefits**. Although benefits can vary greatly by country, there may not be so much difference between the basic benefits offered by different companies in your country. The best professionals are able to choose their jobs, so firms must offer a competitive benefits package. Also, many firms have a full list of various small benefits. The companies readily use them as selling points. They are also a convenient way to draw attention away from the salary. In general, you should not be getting less than colleagues in other companies. So, also find out what kind of benefits are typically offered in your country.

- **Working hours and other terms of employment**. If working hours is an important consideration, you should ask about it. Do it carefully and in general terms, without committing yourself one way or another. For example, you can ask how many hours consultants in similar positions log in general. As a follow-up question, you can ask if overtime is paid. You are probably also interested in flexible work arrangements. Vacation is another consideration if it does not come standardized in your country.

- **Career progress**. It is helpful to know what kind of career path a person in a similar position typically has. If being a manager is your goal, you can ask how you typically grow to be one in the company. Performance management is another critical item to consider. How would your performance be measured? How does it affect raises and promotions? In non-listed companies, ask if there is a possibility to become a partner. It can give a tremendous boost to your career and job satisfaction. In a small company, I would consider such a possibility a must.

- **Work**. If you already know what kind of work you like, it is easy to come up with things you want to know. You can also ask what the interviewer especially likes about the company or their own work. When in doubt, you can ask what kind of role and project you would be first staffed to (they may even have an assignment waiting for you). You can ask about the types of projects and clients. You can inquire about the needs to travel (if it matters to you). If you want to appear knowledgeable, you can even ask about chargeability numbers and rates (but do not expect direct answers). Also, do not forget to ask about the training and coaching provided by the company.

- **Extracurricular activities**. Companies offer activities and opportunities that are not (strictly speaking) benefits but can still impact your job satisfaction. Parties, events, communities, free time activities, and volunteering opportunities are typical examples. If you want to get the discussion to a more informal mode, you can ask about these. Also, do it if you currently do or want to do work for charity.

- **Culture and values**. Ask about anything that is important to you. For example, you might want to know more about the company's equality and inclusion program. If you want to leave an impression (for the better or worse) in an interview, you can ask for practical examples of how the company's values manifest in practice.

Prepare for Surprises

You should be prepared for the unexpected. That is what consultants need to do, anyway. You might be asked difficult or even inappropriate questions. You can be given different exercises to do. You must handle these situations somehow. Winging it is totally fine. So, say something. Anything.

The first thing to do is go through the most typical job interview questions and think of suitable answers for them in advance. There are many listings on the internet you can use. For example, Indeed has an extensive list of questions and answers.

Depending on your country, there are questions they are not allowed to ask you in a job interview. The topics that are forbidden by law may include, for example, family, health, financial status, political and religious views, and sexual orientation. If you are asked about one of these topics, you should politely decline to answer or answer ambiguously—if it feels safe to do so. So check what these questions are in your country. Note that there may be permissible ways to ask about these topics in an indirect way.

The interviewer might want to do a surprise test on your presentation skills. He or she might put you through a similar ordeal that I was. So, just in case, you should be prepared to present some model or framework related to your studies or current work. You may also be given other exercises, such as solving a problem related to a particular case and then presenting your findings. The same advice goes. Do not freeze.

Reflect and Carry On

After the interview, companies take a few days or longer to inform you of their recruiting decision. While waiting for that, spend some time reflecting on what went well and what did not. Thinking about something you might consider a total disaster is, of course, difficult but important anyhow in terms of learning. You will be wiser in your next interview.

Interviewers are also people. And people have a hard time *not* giving any indication of how they think of you in the interview. It might not be too difficult to read these clues from how the interviewer looks and talks. After both of my two job interviews, I was pretty sure that I would be offered the job. Use this information to optimize how you conduct yourself in the next interview. Maybe you will learn, for example, which of your answers were not so convincing.

It also comes down to interpersonal relations. If your interviewer unconsciously dislikes you, it is difficult for him or her to be objective in assessing your suitability for the job. There are also a plethora of other reasons you cannot influence. Maybe the company just began reductions, and all recruiting was canceled. Do not be too hard on yourself if you receive the "thank you but no thank you" message. Learn what you can and carry on.

Do You Really Want to Work There?

Congratulations, you have been offered the job!

Before rushing to sign the work contract, there are still a few things to do. So, take a deep breath, relax, and go through the following checklists.

If you are a fresh graduate:

- Can you meet your goals in the job?
- Does the work time fit your preferences (i.e., not too much work)?
- Does the job look good on your CV?
- Are you able to learn to be a better IT consultant in the job?

If you are changing from your current job:

- Can you meet your goals in the job?
- Does the work time fit your preferences (i.e., not too much work)?
- Does the job meet your most important preferences?

Also, think about how you would organize your life around your new job. Does the compensation meet your needs? Will you work long days? How about commuting, business trips, and your kids' daycare? Will there be more or less holiday? In short, will it work out? And what is your gut feeling about the job?

Remember, you can still say no to the offer if you begin to have major doubts. And before you accept, there is one last thing to do.

Check the Work Contract

Many are probably so glad to get accepted to a job that they just sign the work contract without looking at it too hard. That is a mistake. By signing the contract, you are committing yourself to the terms of employment. Some clauses (for example, those related to confidentiality) may bind you for life. A nasty non-compete clause can halt your job search for months after you resign (even if you leave during your probation period). Although your employer will probably sue you only in extreme circumstances, it is good to minimize the chances of that. So, you would do well to spend a couple of hours going through the contract and sleep over it before signing. Never allow yourself to be rushed to sign. I would also recommend you go through the contract with a lawyer.

Check and understand all the employment terms (for example, compensation, work hours, holiday, sick days, work location, confidentiality, and non-compete clauses). The work contract may also refer to a collective agreement. In that case, you must also check the terms of the collective agreement. Make sure that the terms are what you have been told or agreed on before. The terms should also be the same as you would usually expect from similar companies in your country, or better. There are not too many web resources available for helping you with this, but you will find a few articles from law firms. For example, check the one from LawDepot.

Especially, read the fine print on your work time. Work time, as defined in the work contract, can be a set number of hours per week or day, or left undefined. In the latter case, there can be jobs where the law on work time does not apply—even if maximum work hours are defined by law in your country (your country probably has a specific term for this kind of work hours). I would avoid these jobs because the employer has the right to squeeze whatever number of work hours out of you, as necessary. It also means that you do not get paid for overtime.

In practice, the number of work hours required varies but is definitely higher than the normal 40 hours. I have met IT consultants who worked 50–80 hours per week long-time. Granted, some individuals do not mind working long days if they get compensated for it. So, make sure that your compensation covers those extra hours. I would guess this is not always the case. I have met IT consultants without limits on their work hours getting paid only 300–400 euros more per month than me working 40 hours at maximum.

Also, non-compete clauses can be problematic. It is fine to have a clause against doing competing work while employed at a company. There is probably also a law against that in your country. But the clause becomes a problem if it prevents you from accepting employment in another company for a certain time (for example, six months) after you have resigned. If such a clause exists, you should be well compensated for it. It seriously reduces your liberty. Six months' salary amounts to quite a lot of money. Also, consider other consequences arising from these clauses. If they are written very ambiguously, they may prevent you from owning any shares of competing companies, even if they are publicly traded!

Depending on the local laws, some non-compete clauses may not be enforceable, but that does not prevent companies from putting them into their contracts. So check what the contract says and consider if it is worth the risk.

If you like the company in general but find a specific term unacceptable, you can suggest changes. In some countries and companies, the contract you will get is anyway just the first suggestion and open for negotiation. The better credentials you have, the easier it is to get the terms changed in your favor. In larger companies, however, work contracts can be pretty standard, so you can either accept or move on. But it is worth trying, anyway. Some of the terms you could negotiate include compensation, paid holiday, and non-compete clauses.

Prepare for Your First Job as an IT Consultant

For a person new to consulting, or even working life, starting a career in IT consulting is a big change. As a new joiner, your head is probably full of questions and doubts. There are new methods and tools to learn, colleagues and clients to meet, and expectations to fulfill. Even for individuals with work experience, moving into consulting brings a novel viewpoint to work. In IT consulting, your expertise costs the client a whole lot more than it probably did to your previous employer. For a new joiner, it may feel daunting to be expected to deliver what the client demands for its buck.

It is actually not so bad. Every decent IT consulting company has an onboarding program that teaches the basics you need to know. You probably also get ongoing coaching. Of course, there is much variability in the quality of onboarding you will get in different companies. The largest consultancies have onboarding programs for new hires of different experience levels. Those coming directly from the university are put through a course that teaches what IT consulting is and what is expected of you as a consultant, covering even the absolute basics. Some companies expect you to learn the substance in a client engagement and only cover the essentials from company policies in the onboarding.

If you are a fresh graduate, your first role will be an easy one. You will probably work in a support role. Others will have the main responsibility of the engagement. You will be the person who gets the most easy-to-learn, repetitive, and possibly, boring work. "A monkey's job," as they say. If you are staffed in a larger project, the starting point is that of a junior team member. For example, being a functional tester is a fine role for those new in IT consulting. You do not need any skills that would take a long time to train, just an eye for detail and the ability to follow instructions to the letter. If the project is a large one, it is easy to "hide" in it while you build up your skills. So it is as safe a place to begin your career as any. In smaller engagements, you may be assigned a position of a sidekick for a more experienced consultant—in practice, a glorified note taker.

You will learn a lot in these roles. Not only about your own role but also about IT solution implementation projects in general. So keep your eyes open. If you are eager to learn and perform well, there will be more responsibility for you in the future. But take it easy in the beginning. It is very easy to stretch yourself too much. Do your job well, but do not produce over quality.

While it may sound like they expect a diamond from you, a pile of coal will do (it does not even have to be neatly arranged). In the beginning, your superiors are happy enough for you to produce at least something useful and throw in an original idea or question. Granted, there are also those consultancies that expect you to give them 150 % from the beginning. In that case, you better accept what you signed in for since it will not get any easier in the future.

Experienced hires will, of course, initially get more responsibility. But even they will be paired with or otherwise have access to a more experienced consultant for support. If you have previously worked in a more easy-going position, the pace in IT consulting may feel daunting in the beginning. For any newcomer, the expectations will only arch higher and higher. You will gradually get more responsibility and challenges in your roles. Usually, this is no problem since you will also learn a lot.

If you feel left alone initially (especially experienced new joiners may feel like this), ask for help. An experienced new joiner at Coala commented that we have many practices and assumptions built in the work culture. These are not explicitly communicated to new employees, even though they may be obvious to other employees. So, ask about anything that is on your mind—even if it sounds very basic or even stupid to you. Asking is expected of you regardless.

6. STORIES AND ADVICE FROM THE FRONT LINE

You do not have to believe just me. To give you a more diverse picture of how it is to work in IT consulting and how to get yourself a job in the field, I asked selected IT consultants to contribute to this book. These individuals were as kind as to contribute stories and advice on the topic for your benefit.

So, without further ado, let's let them tell the story!

Anonymous, Lead Consultant at a Medium-Sized Nordic IT Consultancy

I am a quality assurance (QA) consultant, which means that I am responsible for planning and leading quality-related work in clients' IT projects. For me (and also generally speaking) QA and testing are IT jobs where you have a very wide view of the different phases and types of IT projects and programs.

The main deliverables of my work can be quality plans, testing strategy, and testing plans or similar documents. Sometimes, I am also active in planning and executing testing in projects. Also, my roles are close to the project manager when it comes to following budgets, estimating work efforts, and managing risks. Normally, I would work around 70% on the client side, but most of my work could be done remotely.

I think my entry into IT would not have been possible if I did not have a reference from an experienced person already working in the company I joined — Accenture. First, I was a summer trainee, but I managed to do my work in a way that I got a continuation for my contract. Finally, after finishing my master's degree on the side of work, I got a full-time job at Accenture. So, you do not always have to be fully finished with your studies to get an IT consulting job.

As a summer trainee, I got to do the same things as everybody else (I was part of a small onshore QA team, the rest of the QA team was offshore). But there were certainly more peer reviews and sparring for all the things that I produced. That was to ensure that I reached at least the minimum quality criteria of the deliverables to satisfy customer needs and expectations.

After getting a full-time job at Accenture, I spent several years learning the so-called "core competencies of IT consulting," until I got headhunted to a smaller consulting company focusing on QA work done by more senior QA consultants. Before changing jobs, I worked in several roles in multiple projects; onshore test support, test coordinator, change management specialist, maintenance lead, and test lead.

For me, starting a career at Accenture gave me an excellent overview of how things work in IT and established basic principles on how consultants behave and work. I internalized the so-called best practices of consulting into my own toolset to enhance my consulting career.

Now, after working for several years in a smaller consulting company, it feels that I would be ready to start my own company — as I have found out which skills are required for ensuring the quality of customers' IT projects.

Dalibor Petrovic, Business Process Principal Consultant at SAP

I am an SAP SuccessFactors consultant, which means that I am responsible for implementing our cloud application for Human Resources for customers from various industries. In my experience, being a consultant for cloud software means that the way you work is quite different from working on on-premise software projects. One of the major differences is the amount of remote work. About 70-80% of my work happens from my home, because all you need is a computer and a stable internet connection to work on configurations, prepare presentations, etc. While in the past customers insisted on having their consultant do all the work on their premises, the expectations have changed. Customers understand that there is no need for a consultant to work on tasks on-site when these tasks require little to no interaction between client and consultant.

Also, the number of customers you are working with in parallel is relatively large. In my case, it means working with 5–8 clients in parallel. This is partially because a lot of work can be done remotely, and so you are not blocked for a single customer for multiple full days. In addition, there are tasks that simply require only a few hours of work before handing them over to the customer to do their part. Lastly, not every engagement with a client is a full-blown implementation project, but only a short assignment to help fix a certain challenge, explain new functionality, or implement a new feature the customer is struggling to implement on its own.

So, what do I do all day long? It is quite a mixed bag, and that is what I like about it. A typical day may start with a status call with client A who is running an implementation project for which I am the lead consultant. This means that I deliver a status report on our progress, point out risks, and provide advice on potential solutions. After this, I might move on to a workshop for client B who is running an implementation as well. During this remote workshop, I leverage popular tools like MS Teams, Menti, or MURAL to present the software, support discussions around configuration decisions, and capture sentiments, thoughts, and results. Since remote workshops can be tiring, they normally do not run all day long, and so we would typically end in the early afternoon. After that, I might get on calls with or answer emails from clients C and D. To finish the workday with something more relaxing, I would start an online training or look up an article to make sure my knowledge is up to date.

Education is an important part of being a consultant for our cloud products because we are part of a fast-moving environment with lots of innovation and changes happening throughout each year. This encompasses innovations for the modules I work with, changes to modules that have some form of connection and impact on my work, as well as market trends, moves to new approaches and even global events like the current pandemic. In order to stay in the loop, one needs to visit the mandatory product trainings, but also find proper news outlets and information sources like blogs, research papers, etc. While this might sound stressful, it is actually quite energizing because you do not have to do the same job and talk about the same things over and over again. Instead, you get to keep evolving and learning new things throughout your career.

If you asked me what my favorite aspect of being a consultant is, I would say it is the variety of customers I get to work with. It is amazing to see the full spectrum of company cultures, how companies run processes, and how open they are to innovation and change. In this regard, I need to cover the full bandwidth and learn to deal with clients struggling with or resistant to change as well as customers who are at the forefront of the digitalization movement with high expectations and challenging demands.

If you are pursuing a career path in HR but are interested in moving into HR IT, I highly recommend giving it a try. Be curious, be open, and be bold. Just start by making yourself familiar with the software you would like to be a consultant for. Seek opportunities to work with it as a key user to gather practical experience. Ask questions and dig deeper to get a better understanding and when you feel ready, make a move for a consultant role in that area. There are plenty of opportunities, and HR IT is a topic that will not go away anytime soon, in my opinion.

Anonymous, Managing Consultant at a Finnish Boutique IT Consultancy

My career in IT consulting started already more than 20 years ago, when I landed a master's thesis position at an international IT consulting company. Afterward, I was offered a permanent position in the company. I cannot recall the details of the related interviews, but apparently, they went well as my career developed pleasantly from that point on. Naturally, my thesis work offered a positive starting point.

Working in a managerial position at an international consulting company, my responsibilities included participating in the recruitment process of my own business unit. Also, on numerous occasions, I have participated in the orientation of new IT consultants. I cannot recall having any training myself for this demanding job, but in a consulting company, interviews and orientations become part of your job after a certain point in your career.

Inspired by Eetu's book project, I began to ponder what kind of experiences I could share with future IT consultants at the very beginning of their careers. Especially, I thought about the interviews which I have conducted and what have been the factors that have influenced me to either recommend or refuse a candidate. I will try to summarize from my own point of view what to pay attention to when applying for a position as an IT consultant.

In the companies where I have worked, HR personnel has typically conducted the first interview with the candidate. If they have been satisfied that this person could be a potential employee, the candidate has then been called in for the second round of interviews with myself or another colleague asking the questions. Here, I would like to raise a few points, which I have paid attention to during such interviews.

Before the interview, I read the candidate's application and CV. I prefer the compact one slider type of CVs that encapsulate the person's core capabilities and interests in sentence form, as opposed to a boring list of experience. Such lists can be included as attachments, if necessary. The graphic appearance of the document is also worth spending two dollars on, to get a nice template, for example. It improves the chances of getting your CV to the top of the pile. I am generally not impressed by videos or other spectacular multimedia presentations. I feel that these might be more relevant in other industries.

One cannot belittle the importance of the first impression. With modest exaggeration, I would say that 90 percent of the people that I have recruited or selected to go forward in the process have given me a good first impression. It consists of simple things. Look your counterpart in the eye, show interest, and be active. A good first impression may, of course, fall apart during the interview. If the candidate leaves a neutral impression because of nervousness, this can still be turned into a win with a good interview. I weigh roughly 50 percent experience and 50 percent being "a nice guy." Turning a poor first impression into a win is trickier. It can be caused by, for example, lateness or arrogant behavior by the candidate.

Bringing forth relevant experience is an art. I can read the candidate's CV line by line just fine; this is not something the candidate needs to do for me. Instead, I appreciate it if the candidate can construct a logical story of his or her experience so that the listener gets an impression of how that person's experience has developed during years of study and work, even up to the point where the current position would form a logical continuum to this story.

You may also try different ways of showcasing concrete deliverables you have made in the past. However, please do not do as one candidate who mentioned an online service he had been building. He jumped out of his chair, crossed over to my side of the table, intent on showing it to me on my computer. As I had the notes of the interview open on my laptop, I was a bit snappy towards him leaning over my keyboard. He, of course, realized his mistake, but the rest of the interview was quite awkward, and it did not lead to employment in this case.

A would-be IT consultant will, of course, have a very short list of experience. Still, odd jobs delivering newspapers or working at a fast-food joint are worth mentioning without hesitation. Everyone has been at that point sometime in their life. The same may apply if you are changing careers. Maybe it would be a good idea to boldly bring forth some experience of teamwork or management that you could apply and use in your future profession. I have also seen student projects successfully showcased in a CV in the same manner as work experience.

Be prepared for a case. At least the biggest consulting companies' interviews include some type of case exercise. I personally have tortured candidates with pretty straightforward exercises, such as "the client contacted us to get help renewing an online service, how would you go about exploring the issue with them?" It is important to remember that there is no one right answer. Instead, the goal is to see how the candidate thinks and test his or her logical reasoning skills in a surprising situation. One will start to draw the architecture of the online service on a flip chart, and another will approach the issue by charting the business needs. How you approach the issue will tell the interviewer about your way of tackling challenges.

Iiro Hietala, Architect at Taitopilvi

I have been working in the wonderful field of IT for over 21 years, in multiple roles and companies. Companies that make their own products, and companies that sell the skills of their consultants as services, targeting both public and private sectors. In my roles, I have seen the most of it. Working as a software developer (backend and front-end), a solution and software architect, a team lead, a Scrum Master, a supervisor, a recruiter, a mentor...you name it. Currently, I am working as a consultant in a small but growing consultant company. Here are some of the experiences and tips I can share with you.

As already stated earlier in this book, if you are just starting your career as an IT consultant, it might be a good idea to start in a role where someone else handles the managing of the project, customer relationships, and so forth. This enables you to concentrate on the goal that you have set for yourself, such as learning to be a good programmer, with all the software craftsmanship aspects related to it.

As a recruiter, I want to be able to trust you from day one. The interview can be a stressful experience and make you nervous (usually needlessly), but as long as you are true to yourself and open about what you know and what you want to do, it creates mutual trust. The purpose of the whole interview process is to find a win-win scenario between the company and the applicant. If falsehoods are given from either side, they will be out in the open someday, and the consequences vary. You might not be happy in the role if you are struggling to fulfill it. Also, if the role is something else than promised, it will break the trust between the employer and the employee. Again, this is not a good situation in the long run.

To sum up:

- As a recruiter, be honest about what you are offering in the role.
- As an applicant, be honest about what you really know and want to do.

To be a successful technical consultant, you may either specialize in one field, e.g., programming, databases, or perhaps user interface development. Or, you can have a broad skill set in all necessary fields and specialize in one or couple of them, so that you know them by heart. Usually, the larger projects need many skills and roles, such as user experience (UX), user interface (UI), backend, and DevOps specialists. In such projects, it may be a good idea to assign a specialist for each role. It also helps, for example, if a UI developer also knows about backend development and vice versa. This makes it easier to proceed faster as the agreement on the proper software architecture is shared between different roles.

I have found out that the most successful software architects have a diverse knowledge of everything related to working software solutions, from infrastructure and deployments to end-user experience, with backend and possibly integrations and front-end solutions in between. This kind of architects may not necessarily excel in every part, but they have the big picture drawn out in their minds (and hopefully also in diagrams shared with the whole team and other stakeholders).

If you are also creating hardware (such as consumer devices, industrial devices, or perhaps autonomous robots), it adds a lot to the overall complexity and thus to the efforts needed to make successful products or solutions. All the pieces of the puzzle need to be placed together at some point.

To be a successful manager, you need to be a person who is genuinely interested in the well-being of your team and people. If you see people only as resources, you might tend to treat them as such. Good leadership is a different thing than being a manager in writing. With poor leadership and people skills, it might get messy quite fast since the most valuable thing in your company, the people, get frustrated and feel bad at work. Remember that developers and IT professionals are usually smart people and may see through you. You cannot trick them for too long. That will lead to brain-leak out from your company as the best people will leave first. Then you have to trick more people in...the vicious circle is thus complete. Honesty and openness are the key aspects here.

Remember soft skills in collaboration with all stakeholders. We are all just people. Some people try to make themselves look better than they are, perhaps to keep their positions. While this is understandable, it does not help to reach the ultimate goal—customer satisfaction.

As time usually is money, learn to concentrate on the most important things at hand. Try not to context-switch as it will always take time to get back on track with the previous task. Learn to organize your work and manage yourself. Learn to know your strengths and weaknesses. Share your knowledge with others. Communicate effectively. Document your knowledge.

Also, remember to try to enjoy your life! Keep work hours manageable. Do not overwork yourself, as getting out of burnout is no child's play.

As the last point, I will shamelessly bring out one concept I want everyone working in the IT field (and why not also in other fields) to know, for the benefit of us all. The

Teal Organization model. If you do not know what it is, go learn about it on the web.

Anonymous, Managing Director at a Medium-Sized Global IT Consultancy

I could not say that one day resembles another in this field. This is part of the beauty of working in the consulting industry. In my earlier years as a consultant, I used to work 4 out of 5 days on-site, at the customer. Each project and customer was different; the tasks in projects were very varied, from holding a workshop to better understand the requirements of the client to writing a blueprint or testing the system (and the customer requirements) before it went live. Personally, this mix was what glued me to this field. Even after 12+ years, I did not yet have a dull day at work.

In my current roles, I oversee an international team of consultants tasked to provide guidance and support to around 50 global customers operating live instances of SAP SuccessFactors, and I am also the country director of Romania for our consulting firm. My diary is scheduled according to the meetings and calls I need to attend. Also, I am trying to block time every day to allow for more focus time, so I can work on different topics. I keep (a rather long) list of things which I need to do to help streamline some parts of our activities, plan or improve the way we are working with our customers.

Around 70% of my work is spent on meetings and calls. We are very mindful of time spent on internal meetings. However, there are important matters to discuss as part of the senior management team. Here meetings equal discussions and decisions about the way we operate our business. External calls and meetings are discussions with our clients, potential new clients or sales pitches, business partners, and account managers from SAP.

Now, there are a couple of things, which are fairly similar each day. I am generally starting my day at around 7:45 and go through the emails I have received. In parallel, I am checking which call I need to attend directly at 8 o'clock and catching up on the missed conversations on our internal chat program. After my first 2 calls, I generally will try to have a period of 2 hours of focused work where I am working on my emails—which can result in scheduling other meetings or calling colleagues or clients.

In parallel, I am checking the ticketing system and trying to get an overall impression of the status quo: overall number and status of tickets, high-priority or urgent tickets, any tricky topics? Once I get a good impression of the status, I will either continue to work on my open issue list or simply follow my diary and probably go on another call.

During the afternoon, I am usually reserving around 0.5 h for LinkedIn activities. Part of these includes sharing relevant articles for my network and checking on the company profile LinkedIn page. Recently, we have started to increase our social media presence and are now focusing more on social selling; hence maintaining our presence on social media is very important.

Anna Aaltonen, Senior Consultant & Founder at Coala

As an employer, Coala is pretty much the same as others — but in a sense also different. We have to offer our employees the same basic benefits as all the other employers. Differentiating with a missing lunch benefit or a very modest health care package just does not work.

Our employees are specialized experts. They must know more about enterprise architecture than their counterparts in client organizations because after all, we are advising them. So, we must get better experts than the client organizations. This is where it gets tricky. How to lure in a specialist who has a lot of opportunities elsewhere?

Paying the best salary will not guarantee success. A lot of client organizations do not mind paying quite a bit more to key personnel since there are usually only a few of them anyway. In client organizations, the performance expectations of getting that salary are also not necessarily so high. Coala, on the other hand, must sell the consultants' work to others and the price is defined by market conditions. Of course, we invest in our brand and try to jointly emphasize the quality of our experts that way. But that does not change the fact that each consultant still must earn his or her pay.

Our consultants share a passion for architecture, a desire to do it right and in a meaningful way. Our consultants want to work in a team where you can get good quality feedback and advice. Even those in the beginning of their careers can learn to be architects if they have the right attitude. This is enticing to certain applicants. While elsewhere the titles may be grand, a more experienced consultant can guess the reality behind grand promises—that is, boring and pleasureless work.

The person we hire is usually someone we know, preferably through work. When we have a clear idea of their working skills, the decision to hire is quite easy. We just negotiate the terms under which work can begin.

When it comes to applicants, I value a consistent CV. There can be a few holes; I understand that these days it is almost impossible to have a work career without any gaps. More concerning is trying to hide those gaps. A sabbatical after working a few years night and day on a project? Is this person really up to the job? Maybe freelancer or volunteer work in between. Unfortunately, I do not know many people who would do this work for free or even in atypical modes of employment. Occasional jobs as a chairman for a condo. Seriously, these are not jobs! Do not lie, because you will get caught. If you need to add a little color, do not overdo it.

How do you then describe your own skills and work experience? Because we are at the top of our food chain, forget about boasting with your know-how. Less is more; just list the tools, methods, and experience you have on using them in practice. That already tells a lot. Too many superlatives while talking about your experience is likely only to cause apprehensions. The small webshop you built can, of course, be the strategic pinnacle of a digitalization project. Especially if I forget that one of my artisan friends also has one. It is worth remembering that in Finland, self-praise is not socially acceptable, so while on a hunt for a job, it is better to maintain a modest tone.

Completed certificates are an advantage. Our clients pay more attention to those than we do, and in some tendering processes, they can have unexpected value. But remember, we do know how to collect an impressive amount of them. It takes more perseverance than supreme knowledge.

The easiest applicants have a reasonable amount of consulting experience, with the correct set of skills. Then we know that consulting in itself is familiar, and the knowhow is there. In that case, we do not need to discuss these more than that.

The most difficult ones to hire are the so-called seasoned professionals. Experience can be more seniority than actual knowledge with market value. If a major part of your expertise is that you know the right people in your own organization, that does not transfer to other organizations. The same goes for being the "memory" of the organization. Even if it is sometimes useful to have someone who remembers what mistakes were made in an enterprise resource planning system renewal 15 years ago, it is not valuable to us. The salary of seasoned professionals has easily risen to a level that is not easy to achieve elsewhere. At that point, you might want to consider staying in your current job. If retirement is still quite a way away, is a new job with less salary really a worthwhile investment?

There are pros and cons of hiring architects from client organizations. There is good expertise available, and many employees do more than could reasonably be expected for the love of the sport. Our challenge as recruiters is to separate the wheat from the chaff. Depending on organizational culture, it may be possible to spend your days hanging around in meetings and leave your own work to consultants. Because the consultant will not bite the hand that feeds, they may even be liable to unfounded flattery of their counterparts: "that was by far the best technology standard decision!"

Consultants are measured according to their output. Sometimes even by the meter. It takes some convincing to assure the client if the result is a twenty-page summary instead of a hundred-page report. The ability to produce material is key. The skills we refer to include grammar, fluency, logical structure, and the ability to communicate in an understandable way. If you are not proficient in these, the content will be lost in format errors. If you cannot produce enough output of reasonable quality, that is the end of your consulting career. Often this can only be found out during the probationary period.

In the end, I still must mention workplace skills. In all organizations, some things are done in a stupid way. There can be more or less effort to fix them, but it may prove impossible despite all efforts. Not everything is worthwhile to fix; the benefit may be smaller than the expense of fixing it. If you are a perfectionist in the wrong way, "nothing is ever good enough," then no job is right for you. If we, as a small employer, get even a small whiff of that in an interview, we will not proceed with the recruitment. We expect you to have a level of tolerance. You will need it in client assignments.

7. SKIP THE BOOK & LET'S GO FOR SODAS

Getting your first IT consulting job is, of course, just the beginning. Even if you are a seasoned professional, you will have tons to learn. You will get to know the business and learn how to conduct yourself as an IT consultant. You will grow into new, larger, and more demanding responsibilities. There might even be a few surprises along the way.

Maybe you have an idea of what your dream job in IT consulting looks like, or maybe you do not have a clue about it (yet). Somewhere on that road, you will start to understand what you like and dislike in your job and company. It pays to be self-conscious about these things. When you begin to understand what kind of IT consultant you would like to become, you will have a clear goal to steer your career towards.

Your first role is probably not the role of your dreams. You may even spend several years in unexciting or uncomfortable roles before getting into something more interesting. Regardless, this is part of the learning experience and necessary for your growth as an IT consultant. While working in your role, you should always be on the lookout for any tasks, roles, and even projects that may interest you. Accepting new responsibilities — even small ones — may take you closer to your dream job.

Even your current company may be a mere stepping-stone for your consulting career. Keep your goals and preferences in mind and reflect them regularly against the roles and tasks your employer can supply you with. After a year or two, if you feel that your goals cannot be met in your current company, feel free to look for one that is better suited to your needs.

With the best planning and research, your first position may still not meet your expectations. If you uncover anything about your employer that makes you feel uncomfortable, it is best to change sooner than later. Just do not rush immediately into resigning. Rather approach your new job search systematically — as you did for your first IT consulting job.

Also, take care of your market value and your CV. For example, changing jobs every two months does not look good. Take any opportunities you get to develop your skills. Consultants are busy but try to attend a high-quality course or seminar every six months or so. While you are at it, it is also a good idea to get a couple of certificates that are relevant to your specialty.

I wish you the best of luck in finding your dream role in IT consulting!

**Please leave an honest review of the book on Amazon!
I would really appreciate it.**

ACKNOWLEDGMENTS

I dedicate this book to all of my IT consultant colleagues.

This book would probably not be without Sakari Turunen's webinar. Sakari also coached me the whole way of getting this book written and published, which helped enormously. I would recommend Sakari's services to anyone wishing to publish a book on Amazon.

Anna Aaltonen is my trusted advisor at Coala for all things writing and consulting-related. Her excellent advice served to make this a better book. I also want to acknowledge the other Coalas that helped me along the way: Petteri Laamanen, Oskari Forsblom, and Anu Ylä-Pietilä. Elina Erkkilä deserves a special mention for proof-reading and several translations. I am also grateful to Coala Ltd, the company, for the very tangible support that made writing this book possible.

Thank you also Henri Sintonen, Teijo Kelander, Timo Laine, and Jouni Lähteenmäki for ideas and advice in kicking off the writing work and along the way. Warm thanks also go to Iiro Hietala and Dalibor Petrovic for contributing their stories and advice, and beta reading.

I also wish to thank all the beta readers for their valuable time and comments: Merja Almonkari, Ilari Autio, Iulia Guriuc, Arron Higgins, Riikka Huttunen, Aino Jacobsson, Olga Jokinen, Tapani Jämsen, Tuomo Kalliomäki, Janita Kingelin, Nicole Kuhn, Tatu Niemi, Reija Nurmeksela, Samuli Pekkola, Katja Penttinen, Juha Rasi, Eero Saarikoski,

Saku Sikiö (an extra-large thank you!), Senja Svahn, Petri Toikkanen, and Pirjo Valjanen.

Also, numerous others gave helpful comments on various aspects of the book on social media. Thank you all! And finally, I want to thank germancreative for the excellent cover design!

Get your **FREE** IT job search checklist and other valuable resources at ITConsultingCareer.com